"There's no one-size-fits-all solution to the problem of evil and suffering. How could a good God allow such bad things in a world he created? The answer depends on which part of the Bible we read. Indeed, there are different strategies within the Scriptures that deal with the complex problem of evil and suffering. That's the genius of Brian Gregg's approach to the question, what does the Bible say about suffering? He lets the voices within Scripture speak to the problem without treating the Bible as an answer book that solves every riddle."

Rodney Reeves, dean, Redford Professor of Biblical Studies, Southwest Baptist University

"In his remarkable overview of the Bible's teaching about suffering, Brian Han Gregg emphasizes the variety in the Bible's responses to this topic. This is coupled with a warning against getting fixated on one or two of these approaches, which may not be the ones that best provide insight and healing in a specific situation. A rich resource for those who struggle with suffering in their own lives and the lives of others."

William Hasker, former editor, *Faith and Philosophy*, author of *The Triumph of God over Evil*

"Brian Gregg brings the insights of a biblical scholar to the experience of suffering in ways that speak to mind and heart alike. His sensitive reading of the Bible shows that it has a variety of things to say about life's greatest challenge, and each has important things to teach us. Even though no single view fits everyone's experience and suffering is always mysterious, there is one thing we can know for sure—God is always with us, always working for good."

Richard Rice, author of *Suffering and the Search for Meaning*

"In this remarkable book, Brian Gregg explores the mystery of suffering with the mind of a biblical scholar and the heart of a pastor and teacher. The result is a thoroughly scriptural and truly pastoral approach to the problem of pain. As Gregg shows, the Bible doesn't have just one answer to the question of suffering—but it does have answers. This book needs to be read by every pastor, every teacher, and every person interested in learning how to trust God with the answers he gives as well as the questions that remain."

Brant Pitre, professor of Sacred Scripture, Notre Dame Seminary

"Brian Gregg takes up the question of suffering with a full realization that Scripture provides not one but numerous ways of addressing this perennial issue. Examining each of these ways with insight and sensitivity, this book does not attempt an abstract philosophical answer to suffering but a way forward in its wake, a way that is marked by both biblical faithfulness and pastoral sensitivity. Such an approach will be appreciated by many."

Kimlyn J. Bender, George W. Truett Theological Seminary, Baylor University

WHAT DOES THE BIBLE SAY ABOUT SUFFERING?

BRIAN HAN GREGG

IVP Academic

An imprint of InterVarsity Press
Downers Grove, Illinois

InterVarsity Press
P.O. Box 1400, Downers Grove, IL 60515-1426
ivpress.com
email@ivpress.com

InterVarsity Press® is the book-publishing division of InterVarsity Christian Fellowship/USA®, a movement of students and faculty active on campus at hundreds of universities, colleges and schools of nursing in the United States of America, and a member movement of the International Fellowship of Evangelical Students. For information about local and regional activities, visit intervarsity.org.

Cover design: David Fassett
Interior design: Beth McGill
Images: Landscape: © Zoltan Toth/Trevillion
Bible icon: © kolae/iStockphoto

ISBN 978-0-8308-5145-4 (print)
ISBN 978-0-8308-9353-9 (digital)

Printed in the United States of America ∞

Library of Congress Cataloging-in-Publication Data
Names: Gregg, Brian Han, author.
Title: What does the Bible say about suffering? / Brian Han Gregg.
Description: Downers Grove : InterVarsity Press, 2016. | Includes bibliographical references and index.
Identifiers: LCCN 2016011846 (print) | LCCN 2016017083 (ebook) | ISBN 9780830851454 (pbk. : alk. paper) | ISBN 9780830893539 (eBook)
Subjects: LCSH: Suffering—Biblical teaching.
Classification: LCC BS680.S854 G74 2016 (print) | LCC BS680.S854 (ebook) | DDC 231/.8—dc23
LC record available at https://lccn.loc.gov/2016011846

P   22   21   20   19   18   17   16   15   14   13   12   11   10   9   8   7   6   5   4   3   2   1

Y   34   33   32   31   30   29   28   27   26   25   24   23   22   21   20   19   18   17   16

For my parents, Douglas and Judy Gregg.

May every journey lead to God.

Contents

Acknowledgments

No meaningful labor happens in a vacuum. *What Does the Bible Say About Suffering?* would not be the book that it is were it not for the people in my life. Needless to say, they are deserving of my thanks.

I am thankful for my colleagues and students at the University of Sioux Falls who have made the last ten years such a rewarding experience. What a privilege it is to pursue Jesus with such wonderful people! I am especially grateful for the friendship, prayer and support of the theology department: John Hiigel, Christina Hitchcock, James Foster, Dennis Thum, Julie Gregg and former members Kimlyn Bender and John Lierman. I thank God for each of you.

I am thankful for the members of my church, Oak Hills, who are committed to living under God's good kingship.

I am thankful for the team at InterVarsity Press, especially my editor David Congdon, who helped give shape to this book.

I am thankful for my family. Julie, my wife, is my greatest supporter. I am grateful that she sees a better me than I do. She is a true partner. When I consider my children, Eliana and Ian, I am saddened by the thought that they too will suffer. I pray that when suffering comes, they will be drawn into the embrace of their heavenly father.

Lastly, I am thankful for Jesus. I hope he speaks through this book as only he can. I would be lost without him.

1

Introduction

✝

Elizabeth was playing with her two young children on a beautiful summer's day when the doctor called with the results of her test, his voice steady but somber: they had found cancer in her lymph nodes. It was moving aggressively and there was no telling whether treatment would help.

Jennifer was thirteen years old when the visits began. She would lie in bed at night, straining her ears for the sound of footsteps on the creaky wood of the upstairs hall. On the nights that her father came, her blood would run cold. Her body went limp and her mind numb when he pulled back the sheet.

Eric could count on one hand the number of days that had passed in the last three years without the sights and sounds of war filling his mind. The battlefield was long gone but he could still hear the whir of bullets and see the faces of the dead. He couldn't imagine life without anxiety, fear and confusion.

Justin could see quiet desperation when he looked into the eyes of his children. The school year was beginning, and he still did not have a job. There was no money for new shoes, backpacks, pens or folders. The unemployment checks had stopped coming; he wasn't even sure how they would handle lunches.

◆ ◆ ◆

Suffering is one of the great universals of human life. It can strike rich and poor, old and young, strong and weak, good and wicked—no one is immune from suffering. If suffering doesn't play favorites, then everyone must grapple with it personally at some point. For a Christian, the grief, pain and loss associated with suffering are entwined with a pressing question: Why has my God, who is both wholly good and completely powerful, allowed this to unfold? How one answers this question, and the manner in which it is answered, can have important ramifications for the life of faith.

In my first years as a professor of biblical studies at a Christian liberal arts university in the Midwest, I have had the opportunity to hear and share many stories. In hearing those stories, I became profoundly aware of two things: First, no single question emerged as often or with as much raw urgency as the question of God's relation to our suffering. Second, very few of my students had any concrete notion of how they might approach such a question. I have seen many of my students adopt one of three responses: losing faith, having an attitude of resentment or fear toward God or coming to believe that God is impotent over the evil in the world.

Bart Ehrman, a noted New Testament scholar, began his 2008 book *God's Problem* by detailing the sad results of his own wrestling with the problem of God and suffering: "The problem of suffering has haunted me for a very long time. It was what made me begin to think about religion when I was young, and it was what led me to question my faith when I was older. Ultimately, it was the reason I lost my faith." Ehrman is by no means alone. Many men and women of faith have surrendered their commitment to the gospel in the face of inexplicable suffering, finding it easier to rid themselves of God than to navigate the mystery of suffering.

Even if we continue to believe in God, there are dangers. If we are unable to reconcile suffering with belief in a good and powerful God, then perhaps God is less good or powerful than we thought!

C. S. Lewis records something of his own struggles to come to grips with the problem of suffering as it relates to God's goodness in his book *A Grief Observed*. Shortly after losing his wife to cancer, Lewis writes, "Not that I am (I think) in much real danger of ceasing to believe in God. The real danger is of coming to believe such dreadful things about him. The conclusion I dread is not, 'So there's no God after all,' but, 'So this is what God's really like. Deceive yourself no longer.'" Fortunately, Lewis found his way out of despair.

Process theologians, on the other hand, have dealt with the problem by reducing God's power. God may not be able to do anything about the suffering in the world, but at least he is not responsible for it. Rabbi Harold Kushner's book *When Bad Things Happen to Good People* is a classic example of limiting God's power in order to preserve God's character. At the conclusion of the book, Kushner exhorts his readers to come to terms with God's limitations.

> Are you capable of forgiving and loving God even when you have found out that He is not perfect, even when He has let you down and disappointed you by permitting bad luck and sickness and cruelty in His world, and permitting some of those things to happen to you? Can you learn to love and forgive Him despite his limitations, as Job does, and as you once learned to love and forgive your parents even though they were not as wise, as strong, or as perfect as you needed them to be?

◆ ◆ ◆

How then is the committed Christian to understand the relationship between God and suffering? Where is one to look for guidance, insight and wisdom? Any hope of grappling with suffering must begin and end with the biblical witness. Christians are people of the Word. We are convinced that God has disclosed important truths to us through the Scripture. Scripture reveals what God wants his people to know while making it clear that there are limits to our knowledge. It provides the believing community with boundaries of right understanding, guiding us into God's truth. Ironically, many Christians who value the Bible often fail to search out the fullness of its wisdom when faced with the dilemma of suffering. This book seeks to remedy this problem. If God reveals truth through his Scripture, then we should search out what the Bible has to say about suffering.

When we do turn to the Bible, what do we find? The first thing worth noting is how often the theme of suffering emerges. From the Garden of Eden in Genesis to the new creation in Revelation, we find attempts to understand the cause of suffering, find deliverance from suffering, remain faithful in the midst of suffering and understand the mystery of suffering. We may not like the answers we find in Scripture, but we may never accuse it of turning a blind eye to the problem.

Second, there is no easy answer to the problem of suffering. This is hardly surprising given the difficulties already discussed, but it is an important point to make. In some Christian circles there appears to be an expectation that Scripture must always speak clearly with a single, straightforward voice. In fact, an exploration of the theme of suffering in the Bible will require nuance, complexity and mystery. Attempts to flatten the biblical response to suffering, reducing it to a slogan or proof text, only serve to distort the biblical witness.

Third, there is no *single* way forward. The Bible includes a number of different responses to the problem of suffering, and we do ourselves and the Bible a great disservice by adopting a one-size-fits-all approach. Imagine that the biblical witness is a talented choir. Members of a traditional choir are assigned one of at least four parts: soprano, alto, tenor and bass. When the choir performs, some songs are sung in unison—a powerful melody that moves and grows in momentum. The proclamation of the good news of Jesus is such a melody. When it comes to suffering, however, the Scriptures' approach is more like a complex harmony. The convergence of voices weaves a pattern greater than any single melody. There are even moments of dissonance—adding to the complexity and mystery of the music. Certainly we have the ability to pick out a particular line in the music. We can focus in on the altos, for instance, in order to appreciate their contribution; in fact, a full appreciation of the music demands that we isolate and consider the various lines. However, it would be disastrously misguided to assess the music solely on the basis of any single line.

It is critical that we understand this point. Time after time, I have had conversations with people trying to come to grips with the problem of suffering who are stuck on *one* biblical response to the problem: they are only listening to the sopranos! This may simply reflect our desire for simplicity. We often find it easier (and perhaps safer) to internalize a particular explanation of suffering and apply it to the circumstances of our lives and world. However, I am increasingly convinced that there are other factors involved in the inclination to adopt one approach at the expense of others.

Having taught several courses on suffering in the Bible, at the university and at my church, I have noticed that most people naturally gravitate toward one or two biblical responses to the problem of suffering. I found this so intriguing that I began to take surveys at the end of courses. I would list the twelve biblical approaches discussed in class and have individuals identify which of the approaches they found compelling. Several interesting patterns emerged:

1. Nearly everybody focused in on one or two of the biblical approaches.

2. The chosen approaches spanned the various possibilities, with at least one person identifying each of the twelve.

3. When asked to identify why they were attracted to a particular approach, a variety of motivations were provided. Favorite approaches were described as comforting, logical, reasonable, suitably mysterious, hopeful and redemptive.

4. Perhaps most interestingly, they almost exclusively gravitated toward the same approach that they would have identified as their favorite at the *beginning* of the course.

These patterns indicate that our personality, upbringing and life circumstances seem to predispose each of us to appreciate some approaches to suffering more than others.

To return to our analogy of the choir, it would appear that, much like real singers, we are all attuned to sing and hear certain parts more naturally. While there is nothing wrong with having a predisposition, it underscores the need to understand and appreciate the full scope of the biblical witness about suffering. If we fail to grasp the full extent of the "music," it will lead to two negative consequences.

First, it is likely that we will be confronted with suffering that cannot be adequately understood through a single approach. When the complexity of suffering rears its head, we will find ourselves ill-equipped to deal with the ramifications. We will be robbed of the hope, peace or logic in which we found solace, left to flounder in uncharted waters. A fuller understanding of what the Bible has to say about suffering can be a much-needed lifeline in such situations— broadening our perspective and enabling us to make theological sense of our circumstances in a new way.

Second, if we cling to the notion that our own particular conception of suffering represents the fullness of truth, we will be inclined to judge those around us. We will be like Job's friends: certain that our answers are sufficient, unable or unwilling to grasp the mysterious complexity of God and suffering. This would be like thinking that a single tool is effective for every task. We may be convinced that the chainsaw is the perfect tool for every job, but we still look silly trying to hammer a nail with it. Worse, someone might get hurt in the process! This happens in the church over and over again when we jump to dispense "wisdom" and "advice" to those in crisis. Often, we do more damage than good simply because we have failed to consider the crisis in light of the full biblical witness. Instead, we resort to our favorite slogans:

"God is punishing you for your sin. Repent and he will restore you."

"It's all part of his plan. Just wait and you will see his purpose in this."

"Satan is attacking you. You need to pray for spiritual protection against him."

"You just need to let go and let God take care of it. Trust him."

The Bible's approach to the problem of suffering makes it clear that discernment is necessary every step of the way. If the Bible offers a range of perspectives on God and suffering, then we *must* be willing to sort and weigh them when we are faced with difficulty. While it is true that several of these perspectives might be relevant in a particular scenario, it is also true that some of them will *not* apply. Some of the biblical options are mutually exclusive. This makes it even more obvious that we must spend time with Scripture, in prayer and in conversation in order to discern the best way to interpret the suffering involved in a given situation.

A survey of the various biblical approaches to suffering makes it clear that the biblical authors seek to do more than help us understand the *why* of suffering. In fact, in many instances answering the question *Why?* seems to be of secondary concern to the biblical authors. Rather, the focus seems to lie on God's various responses to suffering. What is God doing *through* suffering? What is God doing to *address* suffering? What is God doing to *defeat* suffering? If these are points of emphasis in the Bible, we would be wise to pay attention to them. The reality is that the Bible doesn't tell us everything we might wish to know about suffering, but it doesn't set us adrift either. The Bible simply keeps God front and center. God knows about suffering. God cares about suffering. God is at work in the midst of suffering. God is at work against suffering. God reigns over suffering. God suffers. God will one day declare final victory over suffering.

◆ ◆ ◆

This book presents twelve biblical approaches to suffering. Each chapter begins with a small "appetizer," a brief reflection or anecdote that introduces the subject. The main course of each chapter comes in two parts. The first is an exploration of a single text from the Old or New Testament. This Scripture will help us stay grounded in actual biblical text—and keep us from seeking answers where the text doesn't lead. We will examine the context and background of the text, assess its meaning and significance, and most importantly, listen to what it has to say about suffering. A second section will be devoted to practical reflections on important questions that emerge from a contemplation of suffering in the text. As we proceed, remember that each chapter needs to be read as part of a larger conversation. Since the Bible contains a variety of different responses to suffering, we must be patient, content to let the complex harmony unfold.

Two final words of advice: First, even as we explore the unique contribution of each approach, we must not lose sight of the fact that many of them share an organic connection. For example, a number of the latter chapters (10–13) all grow out of the soil of Paul's reflections on the cross. It is not unusual to find more than one of these approaches present in the same book of Scripture. Sometimes they are even embedded in the same passage. The astute reader will be able to pick out threads of other approaches in the representative texts in this book. There is, then, a degree of artificiality in assessing the parts of the whole separately. After all, they exist in relation to one another in the same way that each line of choral music is intrinsically connected to what surrounds it. At worst, we run the risk of obscuring rather obvious connections. Nevertheless, a deeper exploration of the constituent parts is fruitful and will ultimately enhance our understanding and appreciation of the whole. In the final chapter, I will offer some observations that move the conversation back toward integration.

Second, there are two possible approaches to reading this book. One would be to read the chapters in the sequence presented. The advantage here lies in getting a sense for the organic growth of the conversation about suffering, since the order of the twelve chapters loosely reflects a growing complexity in how the people of God have approached suffering over time. However, each new approach should not be understood as supplanting the previous one. Instead, we have a developing conversation about suffering, with new voices offering new insights over the generations. It is likely that these insights emerged in clusters as products of community reflection and divine action. A second approach would be for readers to begin by entering into conversation with several of the approaches they already find stimulating and meaningful. Identifying and validating these personal "cornerstones" may, in fact, enable you to receive what other approaches contribute with open hands and hearts. In deciding which chapter grabs your attention, feel free to consult the first pages of the conclusion, which contain a brief synopsis of each approach. Proceed with great freedom!

2

The Two Ways

Suffering and the
God of Justice

I have heard many sermons extolling God's forgiveness, love, compassion and grace. I've preached a good many of them myself. But what about the justice of God? When God declares his name to Moses, he goes on to describe his character: "The LORD, the LORD, a God merciful and gracious, slow to anger, and abounding in steadfast love and faithfulness, keeping steadfast love for the thousandth generation, forgiving iniquity and transgression and sin, yet by no means clearing the guilty, but visiting the iniquity of the parents upon the children and the children's children, to the third and fourth generation" (Ex 34:6-7). Like many readers, my inclination is to eagerly embrace the first part of this text and then stop reading before God mentions his commitment to justice. Justice sounds scary! But it is impossible to speak of forgiveness, mercy and grace outside of justice. God's basic commitment to good over against evil is why we, a sinful people, need his mercy to begin with. We have all sinned. What is more, we know what it is to be sinned against. God cares about such things because he cares about us. God's justice might frighten us, but it is ultimately good news—a reminder that God takes sin seriously. Thankfully, God is gracious as well as just.

DEUTERONOMY 30:15-20

[15] See, I have set before you today life and prosperity, death and adversity. [16] If you obey the commandments of the LORD your God that I am commanding you today, by loving the LORD your God, walking in his ways, and observing his commandments, decrees, and ordinances, then you shall live and become numerous, and the LORD your God will bless you in the land that you are entering to possess. [17] But if your heart turns away and you do not hear, but are led astray to bow down to other gods and serve them, [18] I declare to you today that you shall perish; you shall not live long in the land that you are crossing the Jordan to enter and possess. [19] I call heaven and earth to witness against you today that I have set before you life and death, blessings and curses. Choose life so that you and your descendants may live, [20] loving the LORD your God, obeying him, and holding fast to him; for that means life to you and length of days, so that you may live in the land that the LORD swore to give to your ancestors, to Abraham, to Isaac, and to Jacob.

Our survey of biblical responses to suffering starts with the principle of divine reward and punishment. For the Hebrew people, this served as an important baseline for contemplating life's misfortunes. The principle is simple enough: both the good and the bad that befall people are directly the work of God. The good is reward for faithfulness, integrity and obedience. The bad is punishment for sin in its various manifestations. This principle gives rise to a theology of the "two ways." Blessings come to those who follow God, and they reap the benefits of his favor. Those who stray from their maker set their feet on dark paths. They will find only death and destruction—God's judgment on a life lived in rebellion. This judgment might not fall immediately, but its coming is as certain as the character of God, whose justice is its source.

I have chosen a text from Deuteronomy as a principal example of the two ways because there is widespread agreement among Old Testament scholars that the present form of much of our biblical history (Joshua, Judges, 1 & 2 Samuel, 1 & 2 Kings) has a great deal in common with the book of Deuteronomy. In many ways, Deuteronomy contains the clearest formulation of the theology that came to expression in this entire collection of books. Though Deuteronomy undoubtedly contains very old material about the law and God's dealings with his people, there is evidence that the final form of Deuteronomy wrestles with the difficult reality of the exile of Judah in the sixth century BC. This means that Moses' words in Deuteronomy are not merely sage advice for his contemporaries; they also have something to say about the crisis in Judah many centuries later. Deuteronomy and the historical books that follow it tell the story of God and his people in a manner that made sense of their present circumstances in light of their past, while pointing a way forward into the future. By focusing on a text at the climax of the book of Deuteronomy, we are peering into the theological underpinnings of a great deal of the Old Testament. What we find is a theology that is struggling to come to grips with the suffering of God's people in light of exile.

Few events shaped the covenant people of God like the experience of exile. The subjugation of Judah was efficient and brutal. Jerusalem, the city of David, was reduced to rubble. God's holy dwelling place, the temple built by Solomon, was utterly destroyed. The Babylonian army acted without compassion or mercy. The memories of Babylonian cruelty lingered long: "O daughter Babylon, you devastator! Happy shall they be who pay you back what you have done to us! Happy shall they be who take your little ones and dash them against the rock!" (Ps 137:7-9).

But the suffering of exile extended far beyond the death of family members and the destruction of home. It called into question the relationship between God and his chosen people. Had God forsaken his people? Had he abandoned his covenant with Abraham, Isaac and Jacob? All the evidence seemed to suggest that this was exactly what had happened. For one thing, the land of Canaan was a symbol of God's covenant promise and a reminder of God's faithfulness. In the aftermath of the Babylonian conquest, all those with power and influence in Judah were led forcibly to Babylon. They were taken out of the land of promise, the inheritance promised to Abraham, Isaac and Jacob.

God had also made promises to David. "Your house and your kingdom shall be made sure forever before me; your throne shall be established forever" (2 Sam 7:16). Now, there was no king upon a throne in Jerusalem. The Davidic line had been humbled. David's fair city lay in ruins.

Furthermore, Solomon's temple, the very house of God, was destroyed. There would be no worship within its walls, no sacrifices on its altars, no prayers on its steps. The temple was the heart of Israelite worship. Rising high atop Mount Zion, it reminded citizens and pilgrims alike of the holy, wonderful and mysterious presence of God. Its walls were a testament to God's desire to be among his people. It was a poignant reminder that God desired relationship. He was a God who wanted to be known, and he had committed himself to being found in his temple. "I have consecrated this house that you have built, and put my name there forever; my eyes and my heart will be there for all time" (1 Kings 9:3). Now, the house of God was no more.

Why had this horrible series of events transpired? Why was Judah's covenantal relationship with God hanging by a thread? Was there any hope for restoration? Deuteronomy and the historical books that follow provide insight into these questions and others. With one voice these key books assert that *God administered judgment against his wayward people.* God himself roused Babylon to violence. The exile, the loss of a Davidic ruler, the destruction of the temple of God—all of these befell Judah because of sin. Hope, where it was to be found, lay in repentance and covenant keeping. Few passages address these critical questions with greater clarity and power than Deuteronomy 30:15-20.

This passage is situated at the end of an extended reflection on the covenant Israel made with their God. It has the form of a covenant renewal ceremony, a kind of treaty, which characteristically includes the requirements of faithful adherence to the covenant, blessings and curses, and the invocation of witnesses to the agreement. This is seen in Deuteronomy 30:19, "I call heaven and earth as witnesses against you today." In the narrative flow of Deuteronomy, as the people are preparing to enter the promised land, Moses spells out God's covenantal demand that he alone should be the one to receive devotion and obedience. His people must put their trust in him and diligently follow his Torah. The climax of Moses' speech comes in the form of an exhortation to choose the Lord, for only his way leads to life.

The choice Moses lays out before the people in Deuteronomy 30:15-20 does not concern whether the people will accept the terms of the covenant. The people have *already* bound themselves to God in covenant. Nevertheless, they still have a critical choice to make. Will they walk by the terms of the covenant, or forsake their promises? Each of these two ways will lead to a certain outcome. God will respond to faithful obedience with life, but he will punish those who turn aside from the covenant with death.

The passage begins with an allusion to the beginning of the book of Deuteronomy. "See, I have set before you today life and prosperity, death and adversity" echoes the wording of Deuteronomy 1:8: "See, I have set the land before you; go in and take possession of the land that I swore to your ancestors, to Abraham, to Isaac, and to Jacob, to give to them and to their descendants after them." Deuteronomy's audience is encouraged to remember the promises God made and the manner in which he fulfilled those promises. He did indeed bring the descendants of Abraham, Isaac and Jacob into the land of Canaan. The conquest of the land was successful because God remained with his people, fighting on their behalf. Therefore, the choice set before them is an informed one. When God promises life and blessings, he delivers.

Life. The choice that God sets before them is put in the starkest terms. On the one hand, there is "life." Repeated six times in these verses, "life" represents God's good intentions for his creation. It hearkens back to the breath of life with which God awakens the first man, that seminal moment when humankind receives from God something of God's own nature: "Then the LORD God formed man form the dust of the ground, and breathed into his nostrils the breath of life; and the man became a living being" (Gen 2:7).

In our passage, "life" is joined by two other terms that describe God's good intentions for his people. The first is "the good" (*hatôb* in Hebrew), which the NRSV translates "prosperity" in the first line of our passage (Deut 30:15). "The good" is also reminiscent of the creation account. It points to both God's good desires for his creation and the very character of God, who creates only what is good. Significantly, God proclaims the goodness of creation seven different times in the first chapter of Genesis (Gen 1:4, 10, 12, 18, 21, 25, 31). The good has always been God's desire for his creation.

Those who choose the way of the Lord are also twice promised "blessings" from his hand (30:16, 19). These blessings point to God's active role in rewarding those who choose him. The categories of blessing and curse have played a primary role in the material leading up to Deuteronomy 30:15-20. It is clear that these are covenantal blessings and curses. If Israel is obedient to the terms of the covenant, God will bless. If they violate the terms of the covenant, God will curse.

Three further ideas explore the *type* of blessings that God gives. The first is multiplication: "You shall live and become numerous" (30:16). Behind God's promise to multiply a faithful Israel lies the covenantal promise to Abraham. When Abraham was childless, God made a promise to him: "I will indeed bless you and I will make your offspring as numerous as the stars of heaven and as the sand that is on the seashore" (Gen 22:17). The Israelites are proof of God's faithfulness to Abraham. God still desires to bless his people and their descendants, if only they will walk in faithfulness as their forefather Abraham did. Perhaps also in view is God's command to Noah: "And you, be fruitful and multiply, abound on the earth and multiply in it" (Gen 9:7). This moment of "new creation" affirms life and God's desire to see it multiply.

A second blessing that evokes God's promises to Israel's ancestors is the land (30:16, 18, 20). As the final verse makes explicit, the privilege of living in the land of Canaan flows out of God's covenant with Abraham, Isaac and Jacob. If Israel adheres to the covenant, they will "live in the land that the LORD swore to give to your ancestors, to Abraham, Isaac, and Jacob" (30:20).

Third, the blessings include "length of days" (30:20). Long life was considered a blessing of the Lord. Moses himself lived to the ripe age of 120 (Deut 34:7).

The choice for "life," therefore, is summed up in terms that evoke God's good intentions for creation, on the one hand, and God's covenantal promises on the other. Together they serve as vivid reminders of God's ability and desire to bless those who follow him.

What must one do in order to choose life? This choice is described in three ways: "by loving the LORD your God, walking in his ways, and observing his commandments, decrees, and ordinances" (30:16). In the initial command, "love the LORD your God," the entire orientation of one's life is in view. Love denotes devotion, passion and commitment. Israel is called to love neither passively nor partially. The construction used throughout these verses, "the Lord your God," is particularly apt here. God is a person, and Yahweh is his personal name (signified by "the Lord" in most translations). The commitment of love is not made to a generic god; it is made to Yahweh, the *person* who is God. I do not love my wife simply because of her role in my life. I love Julie, the *person* who is my wife. Real love can only exist between persons in relationship. This is the reason God makes covenant with his people. Covenant represents God's deep commitment to relationship.

The second command begins to put flesh on the command to love. Israel is to love God by "walking in his ways." God's character becomes a model for his people. To love God is first and foremost to strive to imitate God. Act as he acts; think as he thinks; love as he loves.

The final command points to the law, God's covenantal instructions to his people. Its various "commands, decrees, and ordinances" must be followed because they reveal to Israel what God desires. The law is one way in which God has graciously demonstrated to his people *how* they might love him and walk in his ways. Obedience to the law flows naturally out of the first two commands.

The choice for life and all that it entails takes precedence in the passage. It is not only the first option placed before Israel; it is also described in greater detail and reinforced at the conclusion of our passage. Nevertheless, it is not the only possibility for the people of God. There is another choice available: the choice for death.

Death. In Genesis, "death" is introduced into God's good creation because of the sin of man and woman. Death is the necessary consequence of sin, but it remains very much outside of God's creative purposes. It is the destruction of God's creation. Just as Adam and Eve chose for death when they spurned God's command in their desire to be like God, so too death will come upon all those who continue to seek a replacement for God, failing to render unto him the love and obedience that are his due. "Life" and "the good" in Deuteronomy 30:15 are paralleled by "death" and "the evil" (*hārā^c* in Hebrew), translated "adversity" by the NRSV. All that is evil, with first place reserved for death itself, is in store for those who live in opposition to God.

Three other ideas fill out the picture of death. First, just as blessings flow to those who live with the Lord, curses are in store for those who choose against him (30:19). These curses come from God and point to God's role in administering judgment. Second, those who turn away are told that they will "perish" (or be destroyed; 30:18). In Hebrew, the point is emphasized with the use of an infinitive absolute, in which the word is repeated in order to drive home the inevitableness of the consequence. An adequate translation would be "you will *certainly* perish." Those who think that they can bypass the terms of the covenant should think again. God will punish those who spurn the covenant. Third, a concrete reminder of what will be lost comes in the form of the land (30:18). Exile looms as the ultimate curse, a clear rejection by God himself. It is the dissolution of the very covenant that held the promise of God-breathed life.

What does it look like to choose death? A threefold sequence in verse 17 spells out the process of falling away: "Your heart turns away, and you do not hear, but are led astray to bow down to other gods and serve them." In stark contrast with the command to love God, the path of death begins when the *"heart turns away."* In Hebrew thought, the heart was the essence of the inner person. To speak of a heart that turns away from God is to speak of a person in pursuit of other things. The emphasis lies on the concrete *choice* of the individual. Once the mind and the will were focused on God; now they have turned away.

The second step is that such persons not only fail to *heed* the call of God, they eventually fail to *hear* it. Their ears become deaf to a message that they have chosen against. They have walked too far down a strange path. There is no turning back.

Finally, the inevitable result is the worship of other gods. Baal, Astarte, Molech—attractive alternatives were ever present in the land. Deuteronomy repeatedly condemns this false worship. It should be noted, however, that the logic of verse 17 suggests that the roots of the problem run much deeper. They lie at the level of the inner person. Just as it was for Adam and Eve in the garden, the root idol is self. It is the desire to be like God, the desire to forge our own destiny, the desire to manipulate spirit and matter to our own ends, the desire to *be* gods.

In Deuteronomy 30:15-20, then, the choice between life and death is extended to the people of Israel. If they love their God, walk in his ways, and observe his commands, decrees and ordinances, they will have life and blessings. If their hearts turn away, and they fail to hear and are led astray to worship and serve other gods, then they will have death and curses. The choice is for the whole nation, but it is also for each individual. In fact, this passage almost exclusively uses the second-person singular. The choice that lies before the people of God begins in the heart of each person in the community.

What Deuteronomy 30:15-20 tells us about suffering is that it comes from God as the divine response to sin. Those who choose against God will be cursed by their rightful Lord. Those who violate the covenant will suffer death, just as the terms of the covenant demand. Why does Judah find itself in exile? Why does the Davidic throne stand empty? Why has the temple of the living God been reduced to rubble? These things happened because of the sin of God's people. They chose death, and God himself visited it upon them. According to the "two ways," suffering is the justice of God in action. It is the divine response to human sin, a corrective and a punishment. Suffering is God's affirmation that good is good and evil is evil; right is right and wrong is wrong.

REFLECTIONS

In the covenantal context of God and his people in the Old Testament, both judgment and salvation were primarily conceived of in corporate terms. God's people would suffer together because of their corporate sin, and they would find deliverance as a people when they turned back to him. Today, for good reasons and bad, we are inclined to a much more individualistic approach to divine justice. I may be uncomfortable with God's declaration that the punishment for Solomon's idolatry will be visited upon his son Rehoboam (1 Kings 11:9-13), but it is unlikely that an Israelite at the time would have had a similar response. Much has changed since the writing of Deuteronomy. Many of Israel's chief identity markers—temple, land, a chosen race—have been dramatically reconfigured by the new covenant established in Christ. We must, therefore, proceed with caution as we seek to apply the two ways in the context of our new covenant reality.

The first thing to note is that the "two ways" is an appealing way to approach suffering in that it renders suffering comprehensible. Suffering is the direct outcome of a just God administering justice. There is something comforting about being able to isolate the cause of suffering in this way. God is invested in punishing sin and rewarding righteousness. When you rebel against God, he visits punishment upon you. Given the elegant simplicity of the proposition, it is perhaps not surprising that this view of suffering was so pronounced in early Hebrew thought. It is not by accident that Psalm 1, which serves to introduce the Hebrew prayer book, lays out the "two ways." The fact that many of the later psalms struggle to see this pattern at work merely reinforces the far-reaching impact of the "two ways."

Happy are those
who do not follow the advice of the wicked,
or take the path that sinners tread,

or sit in the seat of scoffers;
but their delight is in the law of the LORD,
and on his law they meditate day and night.
They are like trees
planted by streams of water,
which yield their fruit in its season,
and their leaves do not wither.
In all that they do, they prosper.

The wicked are not so,
but are like chaff that the wind drives away.
Therefore the wicked will not stand in the judgment,
nor sinners in the congregation of the righteous;
for the LORD watches over the way of the righteous,
but the way of the wicked will perish.

The appeal of the "two ways" extends beyond its ability to make sense of suffering. It also offers the sufferer some measure of control. Presumably, if you know that suffering has come upon you as a direct result of sin, then you can do something about it. God's justice is not like gravity, always and obviously exerting its influence. God may opt for mercy. Suffering can thus be alleviated by making amends with God. On a national level, consider the story of Josiah, the king who received the rediscovered law of God and swiftly moved to set things right: "Great is the wrath of the LORD that is kindled against us, because our ancestors did not obey the words of this book, to do according to all that is written concerning us" (2 Kings 22:13). Josiah's heartfelt response earned Judah a reprieve. On a smaller level, turn to the life of David. The title of Psalm 51, the great psalm of repentance, identifies it as "A Psalm of David, when the prophet Nathan came to him, after he had gone in to Bathsheba." David pours out his heart to God, confessing his dire sins (adultery and murder!) and proclaiming his desire to move in a new direction. Here we see a mingling of justice and mercy in God's response. David receives the forgiveness of God. Not only will he avoid stoning, the prescribed penalty of the law, but he will continue to be king and remain in relationship with God. However, David also loses his son and suffers public shame, another reminder of the decidedly corporate nature of punishment in Israel.

The "two ways" also offers control to those who would counsel the sufferer. In the book of Job, Job's friends press upon him the cold logic of the "two ways." God is just, they tell him, so his suffering must be deserved. To their credit, Job's friends longed for him to be released from his torment and restored to right relationship with God. As far as they were concerned, this power lay in Job's own hands. If only he would repent of wrongdoing, God would restore him.

A further attraction of the "two ways" is that it allows us to distance ourselves from the suffering of others. It insulates us against the randomness of suffering, providing us refuge from the terrifying thought that the suffering we witness could be our own. We remind ourselves that suffering can be avoided by looking to God for protection. The failure of others to do so need not cause us undue fear. Usually this thought process happens on the subconscious level. We need some assurance that our friend's newly diagnosed cancer couldn't just as easily have been our own, or that we were spared the devastating effects of a tornado for good reason when those one hundred miles away lost all that they had. It is easier to sleep at night when we believe there is an explanation for every problem—and we know what the explanation is.

The "two ways" is not just attractive as an explanation for suffering; it is also immensely difficult to rule out as a possible cause. After all, we are all prone to sin. Who can say with certainty that their suffering is not punishment for sin? Even on the far side of the cross, we stagger toward holiness with uneven steps. Our transformation in Christ is far from complete. There is *always* sin for God to punish.

In many ways, the coming of Christ magnifies this problem because he revealed to us the true depths of our sin. With the Torah alone as guide, one might meaningfully assert righteousness before God. For example, Psalm 44:17-22 boldly argues,

> All this has come upon us,
>> yet we have not forgotten you,
>> or been false to your covenant.
> Our heart has not turned back,
>> nor have our steps departed from your way,
> yet you have broken us in the haunt of jackals,
>> and covered us with deep darkness.
>
> If we had forgotten the name of our God,
>> or spread out our hands to a strange god,
> would not God discover this?
>> For he knows the secrets of the heart.
> Because of you we are being killed all day long,
>> and accounted as sheep for the slaughter.

But in Jesus, we are made aware of a new standard of righteousness that embodies God's own character. For example, in the Sermon on the Mount, Jesus says:

> For I tell you, unless your righteousness exceeds that of the scribes and the Pharisees, you will never enter the kingdom of heaven. . . . But I say to you that if you are angry with a brother or sister, you will be liable to judgment; and if you insult a brother or sister, you will be liable to the council; and if you say, "You fool," you will be liable to the hell of fire. . . . You have heard that it was said, "You shall not commit adultery." But I say to you that everyone who looks at a woman with lust has already committed adultery with her in his heart. . . . Be perfect, therefore, as your heavenly Father is perfect. (Mt 5:20, 22, 27-28, 48)

These are hard words. They set before us a standard of excellence that takes its lead from God himself. Moreover, they are indicative of Jesus' teaching on discipleship as a whole. "If any want to become my followers, let them deny themselves and take up their cross and follow me" (Mk 8:34). In Jesus, we see what we have been called to, but we also see how far we fall short. As Paul says, "All have sinned and fall short of the glory of God" (Rom 3:23). And in addition to our personal sin, we are all hopelessly compromised by various corporate and institutional evils. All too often, "the good" for me comes at the expense of "the good" for another. A decision as simple as where to buy shoes may be a matter of justice for someone halfway around the world!

For all of these reasons, it is tempting to assess all suffering in light of the "two ways." For many, it remains the default explanation of suffering, whether this is admitted or not. Too often we act as Job's friends, unable or unwilling to consider other possibilities because they go hand in hand with mystery, powerlessness and vulnerability.

◆ ◆ ◆

However, as the rest of the biblical witness makes clear, there are numerous other ways to understand what God is doing in the midst of suffering, many of which explicitly call the simple logic of the "two ways" into question. For example, many texts from the Wisdom literature, particularly Job and many of the psalms, challenge the basic cause-and-effect paradigm of the "two ways." In John 9, Jesus famously corrects his disciples' erroneous assumption that a blind man owes his condition to sin: "As he walked along, he saw a man blind from birth. His disciples asked him, 'Rabbi, who sinned, this man or his parents, that he was born blind?' Jesus answered, 'Neither this man nor his parents sinned; he was born blind so that God's works might be revealed in him'" (Jn 9:1-3).

It is my hope that this book's exploration of twelve biblical texts, each with its own contribution to the question of suffering, will enable us to put the "two ways" in proper perspective. It would be imprudent to seek to explain the nature of all suffering via the "two ways." The fact is that not all suffering is the justice of God at work.

This truth is particularly important for American Christians to internalize. We increasingly live in a culture that eschews complexity in favor of stark black-and-white thinking. One of the more prominent ways this finds expression is in the assumption that, by and large, people get what they deserve. But thanks be to God that he does not always treat us as we deserve! God is a God of grace who seeks to restore and redeem his wayward creations. The atoning death of his son bears witness to the reconciling heart of God. While we were still enemies, he died for us. Since God loves his enemies, he desires that his followers do likewise. This alone should give us pause in our rush to conclude that all the suffering we see around and within us is God's judgment on sin. As we will see, the potential for damage to self and others is enormous if the "two ways" is all we have to work with.

Those prone to interpret all suffering in light of the "two ways" are subject to some particular problems. To begin with, God is known and related to primarily as a judge, the great enforcer of moral absolutes. Sadly, this reduces the character of God to *one* of his attributes, prioritizing it above everything else to such a degree that God becomes two-dimensional—little more than justice personified. This is unfair to both God and us, since it misrepresents God and erects a barrier to knowing him. Far too many Christians relate to God as though he has a club poised over his head, waiting to strike the offender. I am reminded of Tom, a young pastor whose wife began to exhibit disturbing behavior, leading to her arrest for lewd public conduct. It took some time and counseling to diagnose a bipolar condition, and several more months to determine effective drug dosage. Tom was heroic during this period, maintaining his pastoral duties and shouldering complete responsibility for his children, all while seeking the health and healing of his wife. But most difficult of all was the private hell Tom went through. He was convinced that he must have done something to arouse the wrath of God, and tried to determine what he had done to deserve "God's punishment." If only he could discover what it was so that he might repent and be restored into right relationship with God. But as Tom eventually came to see, God wasn't against him; God was with him in his care for his wife and children. In many ways, the gospel message seeks to liberate people from this kind of fear, juxtaposing life in the Spirit with life under the law. As Paul reminds the Roman congregation, "You did not receive a spirit of slavery to fall back into fear, but you have received a spirit of adoption" (Rom 8:15).

The person who overemphasizes the "two ways" is also liable to cultivate an unhealthy introspection. If you are convinced that your suffering is the result of sin and no sin is readily apparent, you will continue your search for sin until you find the "cause" of your affliction. This search can lead to a systematic second-guessing of motives and thoughts that, rather than bringing clarity, can lead to paralysis. The attempt to parse every action and reaction, every desire and impulse, every idea and intention can only lead to despair. If the fault cannot be found in sins of commission, you can always turn to sins of omission. You may throw open the doors to speculation about what you have failed to do for God that has earned his wrath. This path is both crippling and destructive. Ironically, this ever-increasing introspection leads away from God, shifting the focus from what *he* has done, is doing and will do, to what *we* have done, are doing and will do. Instead of taking our place in God's story, we have made our own faults and shortcomings the measure of all things, exaggerating their significance—and our own importance.

An overemphasis on the "two ways" can also lead to a posture of judgment toward the sufferer. When we think that suffering is *deserved*, we are far less inclined to extend mercy and offer aid. After all, if it is God's hand at work, who are we to second-guess God? So we remain detached and aloof, watching suffering play out in the lives of others from our position of moral superiority. An example of this came on September 18, 2006, where prominent pastor John Hagee expressed his views on Hurricane Katrina in an NPR interview with Terry Gross.

> All hurricanes are acts of God, because God controls the heavens. I believe that New Orleans had a level of sin that was offensive to God, and they are—were recipients of the judgment of God for that. The newspaper carried the story in our local area that was not carried nationally that there was to be a homosexual parade there on the Monday that the Katrina came. And the promise of that parade was that it was going to reach a level of sexuality never demonstrated before in any of the other Gay Pride parades. So I believe that the judgment of God is a very real thing. I know that there are people who demur from that, but I believe that the Bible teaches that when you violate the law of God, that God brings punishment sometimes before the day of judgment. And I believe that the Hurricane Katrina was, in fact, the judgment of God against the city of New Orleans.

The ease with which Hagee draws conclusions about the punishment of New Orleans should make us uncomfortable. He doesn't claim prophetic insight, yet he knows the exact cause of the judgment? Would he really be willing to draw the same conclusions in every case of tragic destruction because "God controls the heavens"? Is it the judgment of God when a tornado levels a small town in Kansas or an earthquake deals out death in the suburbs of Los Angeles? Does each similar event ultimately point to the wrath of God?

We should be skeptical of this line of reasoning. Jesus died in order to reconcile a sinful people to the Father. His grand rescue operation is still very much under way. He calls all people to himself, including those deemed wicked. When Jesus was asked why he dined with tax collectors and sinners he responded, "Those who are well have no need of a physician, but those who are sick; I have come to call not the righteous but sinners" (Mk 2:17). Jesus taught his followers to "love your enemies and pray for those who persecute you, so that you may be children of your Father in heaven; for he makes his sun rise on the evil and on the good, and sends rain on the righteous and on the unrighteous" (Mt 5:44-45). In reality, we are *all* deserving of God's judgment. God has cause to destroy every single one of us, but the crucifixion and resurrection of Jesus declare a different purpose—God's purpose to save, to rescue, to deliver. Certainly he is working out his purpose in New Orleans as well, extending second chances, transforming lives, and hoping to draw people to himself. While I can't know for certain that God did not send Katrina as punishment for sin, it seems to me that in his eagerness to point fingers Hagee loses touch with God's deepest purpose. In doing so, he makes the same mistake as the Pharisees, who saw Jesus' ministry as scandalous because he offered new hope to those who were deemed unworthy of it. They longed for personal vindication and judgment of the wicked. God longed for redemption.

In spite of these difficulties and dangers, we cannot ignore the fact that occasionally texts in the New Testament depict God actively punishing wickedness. In the book of Acts, for example, God strikes Ananias and his wife Sapphira dead because they lied to the apostles about the proceeds gained from the sale of their land (Acts 5:1-11). In 1 Corinthians, Paul rebukes the congregation for desecrating the Lord's Supper, and is even willing to talk about God's punishment in corporate terms. He insists that their selfishness and division at the sacred meal have brought the judgment of God upon them: "For this reason many of you are weak and ill, and some have died" (1 Cor 11:30).

Other New Testament texts continue to express the themes of judgment and accountability, but shift the judgment into the future. Paul warns the Galatian Christians, "Do not be deceived; God is not mocked, for you reap whatever you sow. If you sow to your own flesh, you will reap corruption from the flesh; but if you sow to the Spirit, you will reap eternal life from the Spirit" (Gal 6:7-8). Jesus ends the Sermon on the Mount by emphasizing the importance of walking in obedience to him: "The gate is narrow and the road is hard that leads to life, and there are few who find it. . . . You will know them by their fruits. . . . Every tree that does not bear good fruit is cut down and thrown into the fire. . . . Everyone who hears these words of mine and does not act on them will be like a foolish man who built his house on sand . . . and great was its fall!" (Mt 7:14, 16, 19, 26-27).

Most commonly, the judgment of God seems to flow naturally from the choice to sin. The man who commits adultery reaps the consequences of his infidelity: broken trust, estranged relationships, isolation from family. The woman who uses heroin suffers the consequences of her addiction: deterioration of body, loss of self-respect, alienation from others. This conforms to the pattern laid out by Paul at the beginning of Romans, where he indicates that God "gave them up" to the consequences of their sin (Rom 1:24, 26, 28).

If we acknowledge both that the "two ways" continues to play a role in understanding suffering and that the "two ways" does not adequately address every circumstance of suffering, then how are we to recognize when our suffering results from sin? The task is not particularly difficult when the suffering in question represents the natural consequences of sin, but discerning when God is actively punishing sin is much more problematic.

In this situation, I think some basic observations might steer us in the right direction. First, it would seem that the particular sin should be both obvious and significant. God is not interested in sending us on a wild goose chase in pursuit of our error. When parents hand out punishment, the source of error should be crystal clear if they are to be perceived as just. God is likewise invested in making sure we know exactly why we are being punished. When God prepared to judge his people under the old covenant, he sent them his prophets. God was eager for his people to know his heart and his mind. The prophets spelled out in no uncertain terms the sins of his people, their need for repentance and the judgment that would follow if repentance was not forthcoming.

Second, it seems safe to say that the punishment we see God deal out in the Scriptures resulted from egregious sin. There is a sense of proportionality one can rightfully expect from God—the punishment should fit the crime.

Let's take King David as an example of these two points. When David sinned by committing adultery and murder, God sent the prophet Nathan to speak truth to him. Nathan explained the manifold judgment that would fall upon David because of his great sin:

> "The sword shall never depart from your house, for you have despised me, and have taken the wife of Uriah the Hittite to be your wife. Thus says the LORD: I will raise up trouble against you from within your own house; and I will take your wives before your eyes, and give them to your neighbor, and he shall lie with your wives in the sight of this very sun. For you did it secretly; but I will do this thing before all Israel, and before the sun." David said to Nathan, "I have sinned against the LORD." Nathan said to David, "Now the LORD has put

away your sin; you shall not die. Nevertheless, because by this deed you have utterly scorned the LORD, the child that is born to you shall die. (2 Sam 12:10-14)

God was not interested in playing games with David. Rather, he spelled out the coming judgment in no uncertain terms. In addition, there was obvious correspondence between the nature of the sin and the judgment.

Finally, it is worth noting that the number of such judgments in the New Testament is actually quite low. This does not represent a diminishment of God's commitment to justice. Rather, the locus of judgment has principally shifted to a final accounting when the righteous are vindicated and the wicked punished.

3

Sin Is Lurking at the Door

Suffering and Choice

My wife and I both grew up in big cities. When we moved to Sioux Falls, South Dakota, we knew we would be giving some things up. What we didn't know was how much we would like the community. Sioux Falls is large enough to feel like a community on the move, full of new opportunities. At the same time, it is small enough to encourage a sense of ownership. It doesn't feel like the city you live in; it feels like *your* city. Like every community, Sioux Falls has problems. Even so, the problems don't feel larger than life. There remains a palpable sense that choices to serve and engage really make a difference in the larger community.

In October of 2015, a troubled sixteen-year-old in Harrisburg, a satellite community of Sioux Falls, asked to be excused from class. He collected his backpack, strode into the principal's office, aimed a gun at him and fired. Fortunately, there were no fatalities. The bullet slammed into the principal's elbow, but the wound wasn't life-threatening. The young man was tackled by the vice principal and never got off another shot. I was flabbergasted. How could this happen? How could it happen here in *my* community? I have many friends who live in Harrisburg. I couldn't stop thinking about how much worse things could have been. As further details emerged, it came to light that the boy had several additional clips of ammunition in his backpack. There could have been a bloodbath. It felt unreal, unimaginable.

The story barely cracked the national news. A few days later, ten died at a school shooting in Oregon.

Genesis 4:1-8

> [1] Now the man knew his wife Eve, and she conceived and bore Cain, saying, "I have produced a man with the help of the LORD." [2] Next she bore his brother Abel. Now Abel was a keeper of sheep, and Cain a tiller of the ground. [3] In the course of time Cain brought to the LORD an offering of the fruit of the ground, [4] and Abel for his part brought of the firstlings of his flock, their fat portions. And the LORD had regard for Abel and his offering, [5] but for Cain and his offering he had no regard. So Cain was very angry, and his countenance fell. [6] The LORD said to Cain, "Why are you angry, and why has your countenance fallen? [7] If you do well, will you not be accepted? And if you do not do well, sin is lurking at the door; its desire is for you, but you must master it." [8] Cain said to his brother Abel, "Let us go out to the field." And when they were in the field, Cain rose up against his brother Abel, and killed him.

A second important approach to suffering involves suffering that enters into the lives of others through the choice to sin. This approach walks hand in hand with the "two ways" insofar as both assume that God created us with the ability to make good and bad choices. The "two ways" focuses on God's judgment of sinful choices, but that is only half the story. In fact, most sin has destructive consequences that reach beyond the perpetrator. When Anna and Steve divorce, the suffering extends to the children and family. When Laurie is informed by the doctor that she will never walk again, she knows exactly what the drunk driver took from her. As Liz contemplates a new relationship, she prepares herself to deal with the pain of a childhood haunted by abuse. How are we to understand the suffering inflicted on us by others?

The story of Cain and Abel graphically describes the consequences of evil choices. Both Cain and Abel make offerings to the Lord. Cain brings an offering of the fruit of the ground, while Abel brings the fat portions of the firstlings of his flock. God looks with favor on Abel's offering, but he has no regard for Cain's offering. The text provides no explanation for God's favoring one sacrifice over the other. The reader is left uncomfortably aware that, just as God values our freedom of choice, so too will he exercise his own freedom. Cain is enraged by God's decision. He feels scorned. His resentment threatens to overwhelm him.

In a pivotal interchange, God then makes clear to Cain the choice that lies before him. "Why are you angry, and why has your countenance fallen? If you do well, will you not be accepted? And if you do not do well, sin is lurking at the door; its desire is for you, but you must master it" (Gen 4:6-7). Cain can still experience God's favor. God has assured him as much. He need only learn from the situation and respond appropriately. But that is not an easy choice to make. As God says, sin is lurking at the door, encouraging an altogether different response. Cain must master his anger, resentment and shame. He is faced with a choice to let them go or to be controlled by them.

The path Cain chooses is clear enough. He lures his brother into the field and strikes him dead. There is no doubt about who is responsible. God went so far as to spell out the gravity of the choice that lay before Cain, urging him to turn away from sin. Cain has exercised his free will, and as a consequence his brother lies dead in the field. Yes, there will be punishment for Cain, but what about Abel? His suffering was not of his own choosing. It resulted from the sinful choices of another. This is what is so staggering about free will. When we are sinned against, we don't reap what we sow.

REFLECTIONS

Our reflections on suffering as it relates to this passage must begin with an exploration of free will. The triune God has always existed in community as Father, Son and Holy Spirit. From before there was time God has known what it is to love. Out of this love he created human beings, the climax of his creation, in his image. They were created for relationship with him and with each other. God has much to gain by granting free will to his prize creation. The love, worship, trust and intimacy he hopes for must be freely rendered. In order to reap the benefits of real relationship, he must leave the door open for humans to choose against relationship.

It is telling that God places the tree of the knowledge of good and evil in his good garden. This tree represents a tangible place to choose against God. For better or worse, God takes our choices seriously. He honors them—good and bad. The Bible consistently depicts God's willingness to let these choices unfold, even when sinful choices bring harm upon oneself—or worse yet, those who are blameless. I must admit that I am amazed at the vulnerability of God. In creating beings with the freedom of choice, he made space for all that is good, but he also opened himself up to tremendous pain. It is a pain we too experience, since we all suffer the consequences of sin.

Each of us has known firsthand what it means to suffer because of someone else's sin. We have all been victims of the evil choices of others. Evil words and actions have left their mark upon our hearts, minds and bodies. One of my students survived a situation of escalating tribal warfare in the Congo, escaping with his family to the United States as refugees. His stories of ethnic hatred and violence are deeply disturbing. He lived in terror, fueled by constant gunfire and the threat of murder. He was forced to flee from his home, his relatives, everything he knew. For months his family lived on the run, hiding out in abandoned schools, fearing that each day might be their last. To this day he struggles with a deep anger. He is angry at the men who committed such horrible deeds, but he is also angry at God, who did nothing to stop the sin that unfolded.

Yet not one of us is innocent. We too have played the role of sinner, harming others with the choices we make. Sin lurks at each of our doors. We, like Cain, must battle our fear, insecurity, shame, resentment and anger. Failure to master these things often creates suffering for others.

These evil choices and their consequences are the cost paid by God and his creation for his unwillingness to compromise our free will. God, who is just, allows injustice to take place, and suffering multiplies. It may seem cruel, but for God there is much at stake. If he were to compel righteousness, our freedom would be an illusion. Therefore, he lets us sin and be sinned against, so that we might also freely love and worship and serve.

However, as a means of understanding why God allows suffering, free will has some serious difficulties. First, though God seems remarkably invested in maintaining our free will, he also intervenes in the lives of his people. He answers prayers. He delivers from hardship. He brings about punishment. The biblical witness is uniform: God does not passively allow human actions to run their course. God is an active participant in the drama of history. The puzzle, then, is how to make sense of God's frequent inactivity in the face of suffering. If God can and does respond to the choices we make (without violating our ability to make them), why does he not always do so?

Would our freedom be compromised if God answered every good deed with immediate reward and every bad one with immediate punishment? We would be little more than lab rats conditioned by positive and negative reinforcement. If each good choice immediately and invariably yields a tasty treat and every bad choice immediately and invariably yields an electric shock, then any assertion of real choice is shallow at best. This is not how God will draw people into his kingdom, because it does not take seriously what kind of people they are. Rather than having won hearts and minds for himself, God will have accomplished little more than behavior modification. So how does God decide when and where to intervene? Here, God's own freedom seems to be scandalously on display. Much like his seemingly arbitrary choice of Abel's sacrifice and rejection of Cain's, God is free to choose when and where he will act.

A second difficulty with free will involves the question of how "free" our choices really are. We don't all approach the choices we make from a level playing field. A host of issues are in play every time there is a choice to sin. These factors do nothing to excuse sin that results in suffering, but they do remind us how deeply the sickness of sin permeates this broken world.

One factor affecting our choices is our biology. Our legal system recognizes this. The insane, mentally challenged, and children are all held responsible for their (sometimes quite heinous) actions in a different manner from a "normal" adult. But what is normal? What about those who are predisposed to alcoholism or depression? What about those who find themselves on the fringes because of physical, behavioral or learning disabilities? Fair or not, biology affects our choices.

Circumstances also affect our choices. One person's circumstances may encourage a particular sin while those of another make the same sin highly unlikely. It is not by accident that many of those who inhabit our prisons are from lower socioeconomic backgrounds. They live in a system that rarely cares what happens to them. They live without hope of a better future for themselves or their children. They live without any assurance of safety or provision. Should we be surprised that these circumstances lead to increased theft and violence? How are any of us to know what we might do if placed in similar circumstances?

As an undergraduate, I majored in history. One of my primary interests was the rise and fall of the Third Reich in Germany. I wanted to know how such evil was possible. In the course of my research I had a sobering realization: there is no guarantee that I would have responded differently if I were a German youth in the 1930s. What if my parents and community reinforced hatred and division? What if I grew up longing for redemption from the poverty and shame inflicted by the First World War? The schools, the churches, the government, the economy—all were factors that fostered a situation where the great evil of genocide was made possible.

Finally, our past experiences affect our choices. Any psychologist will affirm the formative influence that past experiences have on the choices we make. Phil was twenty-eight years old when he hit his wife. Their argument was fierce and he lost control, sending her to the floor with a blow to the face. Immediately he saw an image of his father standing regretfully over his mother. He was filled with despair. How had he become what he so hated? Our past experiences do not excuse our choices, but we would be naive to think that the tendrils of sin don't reach out to us from the past, seeking to define our present. For example, many studies have demonstrated that tragically, children who were victims of abuse are more likely to become abusive as adults.

Remember the youth from Harrisburg? I can't help but wonder what circumstances affected his decision to shoot the school's principal. What was his life like? Were there key social, psychological and biological factors that might help us to understand why he crafted his terrible plan?

A number of times in the past few years, I have had similar conversations about suffering in which my dialogue partner confidently stated, "Suffering happens because of free will." The look that followed communicated that there was nothing more to say. The fact is, free will does not answer all of our questions about suffering. In some ways it opens up even greater mysteries. Nevertheless, it remains clear that the Bible puts an immense amount of emphasis on the capacity of human beings to make choices and the importance that they make good ones. This is why the "two ways" is so foundational to true wisdom in Hebrew thought. Reward and punishment will ultimately be allotted according to those choices, underscoring their intrinsic relevance. Sadly, the choices we make often lead to suffering.

4

The Purposes of God

Suffering and the
Sovereignty of God

It was the first day of chemotherapy. Lisa's stomach was tied in knots as she settled into the chair for the first time, wondering how her body would respond to the poison about to be drip fed into her veins. It was one month to the day since she was diagnosed with leukemia. No one had really come to grips with it yet. Lisa felt like it was all happening to someone else. The thought of leaving her husband and young daughter made her ill.

Jodi arrived before the treatment got underway. She bustled into the room with a small basket in her right hand and a blanket slung over her left arm. With a tentative smile, she produced some crackers and cheese from the basket and set them on the table. Then she took the blanket and draped it over Lisa's lap, exposing a beautiful elaborate pattern woven in scarlet, navy and forest green.

"Lisa, I know that what lies ahead of you is challenging, but I want you to remember that God is in control. His plan is so much bigger than you and me. If we could just see things the way he does, we would understand how all the pieces fit together. Then we might see clearly how leukemia is part of his plan. Look at the blanket on your lap. If you focus your attention on a small enough portion, the pattern is totally obscured. But look at how beautiful it is when you can see the whole thing."

The door eased open and the nurse poked her head around the corner. "Are we ready to get started?"

GENESIS 45:4-8

> [4] Then Joseph said to his brothers, "Come closer to me." And they came closer. He said, "I am your brother, Joseph, whom you sold into Egypt. [5] And now do not be distressed, or angry with yourselves, because you sold me here; for God sent me before you to preserve life. [6] For the famine has been in the land these two years; and there are five more years in which there will be neither plowing nor harvest. [7] God sent me before you to preserve for you a remnant on earth, and to keep alive for you many survivors. [8] So it was not you who sent me here, but God; he has made me a father to Pharaoh, and lord of all his house and ruler over all the land of Egypt.

A third approach to suffering focuses on the power and authority of God in relation to suffering. If God is sovereign, as most Christians affirm, then everything, including suffering, is under his authority and nothing happens that he does not intend or permit. But theologically, the gap between "intends" and "permits" is a virtual chasm. What, then, does it look like for God to be "in control?" How does he exercise his power and authority? Is God ultimately responsible for everything that transpires, weaving it all together into a seamless divine plan?

A provocative example of struggling to understand the sovereignty of God can be found in the narrative of Joseph and his brothers at the end of Genesis. It is a classic story, full of twists and turns, told in rather straightforward narrative fashion. It is nearly devoid of theological reflection until the climactic chapter, when

Joseph's self-revelation is accompanied by a theological framework for understanding the entire narrative.

The story begins in Genesis 37, when Joseph is 17. Joseph is the first of two sons born to Israel's beloved wife Rachel in Israel's old age. Israel dotes on Joseph, showing him favor: "Israel loved Joseph more than any other of his children" (Gen 37:3). Not surprisingly, the ten older brothers despise Joseph because of Israel's undisguised favoritism. Joseph does nothing to alleviate the tension. He relays to them two dreams in which his family members bow down before him, adding fuel to the fire of their resentment. Joseph's brothers then sell him into slavery and set about convincing their father that his precious son has been eaten by a wild animal. Joseph ends up in the possession of Potiphar, an officer of Pharaoh in Egypt. He thrives in Potiphar's employ until Potiphar's wife becomes smitten with the handsome Joseph. After spurning her advances, she accuses him of attempting to lie with her. Joseph is summarily thrown into prison, where he finds favor with the jailer. While in prison, Joseph's God-given gift for discerning the meaning of dreams helps him to accurately interpret the dreams of two fellow prisoners. In due time, Pharaoh himself is in need of someone to interpret his dreams. He summons Joseph, who explains to Pharaoh that seven years of plenty will be followed by seven years of famine. The dreams were given so that the kingdom might use the years of prosperity to prepare for the coming calamity. Remarkably, Pharaoh places Joseph in a position of authority to execute the plan. Just as Joseph predicted, seven good years are followed by a severe famine.

When the famine reaches the land of Canaan, Joseph's brothers journey to Egypt in the hope of purchasing food. They meet with Joseph, who does not immediately reveal his identity to his estranged brothers. Rather, through a series of tricks he tests their devotion to their father and youngest brother, Benjamin, the other son of his mother Rachel. Having secretly planted a goblet in Benjamin's sack, Joseph accuses his brother of stealing. He must stay in Egypt and pay for his crime. Another brother, Judah, cannot bear the thought. He has pledged to protect Benjamin and he knows that returning to Canaan without him would be a grief too great for his aging father to bear. He pleads with Joseph, speaking to him about Rachel's other son (Joseph) who has already perished, bringing sorrow to their poor father. Judah asks to take upon himself the punishment that is due to Benjamin.

This disclosure and act of kindness prove too much for Joseph to bear. In a flood of tears he makes known his identity. Naturally, the brothers are greatly dismayed. Not only is their brother whom they had cruelly forsaken alive, he has become a great figure in Egypt. Moreover, he now holds the fate of the whole family in his hands. The stage is set for the climax, and it is at this point that the Joseph narrative becomes most explicitly theological. Joseph's words of comfort and wisdom in Genesis 45:4-8 invite the reader to perceive the entire story in a new light.

Joseph begins by reasserting his identity and offering words of assurance: "I am your brother, Joseph, whom you sold into Egypt. And now do not be distressed or angry with yourselves." He makes it plain that they have nothing to fear from him. The time for tricks is past. There will be no punishment for their misdeeds; they will now see his mercy. Moreover, he does not desire for them to lose themselves in guilt. Joseph has come to understand the circumstances of his life in a new way, and he intends to share this liberating perspective with his brothers.

Joseph's brothers need not be overcome with fear or guilt because, even though their sin was indeed terrible, *God* was at work in Joseph's story in order to fulfill *his* purposes. Three times Joseph makes this assertion, recasting his story in light of God's redemptive activity.

First, in 45:5b Joseph states, "God sent me before you to preserve life." The selling of Joseph by his brothers has become the
sending of Joseph by God. God, who gave the young Joseph dreams
about a future position of authority, had fulfilled this destiny
through the wicked act of his brothers. He had not done it for
Joseph's sake, but for the sake of life. With God's direction and
wisdom, Joseph acted to preserve life—for the Egyptians, for the
surrounding lands, and ironically, for his own family in far-off
Canaan. This is the most general of the three assertions, affirming
God's stance toward his creation.

In 45:7, Joseph narrows his focus: "God sent me before you to
preserve for you a remnant on earth, and to keep alive for you many
survivors." This time the work of God in sending Joseph to Egypt is
depicted in covenantal terms. God's promises and purposes for his
covenant people, the descendants of Abraham, Isaac and Jacob,
were threatened by the coming famine. Joseph becomes God's instrument to preserve his covenant people. The twin terms, *remnant*
and *survivors*, both connote escape from a terrible fate (compare
Ex 1:5; 2 Sam 14:7; 2 Kings 19:31).

The third assertion, in Genesis 45:8, is the most explicit of all. "So
it was not you who sent me here, but God; he has made me a father
to Pharaoh and lord of all his house and ruler over all the land of
Egypt." The horrible sin of Joseph's brothers surrenders to the redemptive work of God, who accomplishes his own purposes
through their act of treachery. Looking back, Joseph can see God
at work on his behalf even when things seemed darkest. *God*
wanted Joseph in Egypt. *God* made him a father to Pharaoh and
lord of all his house. *God* revealed Joseph's destiny to him in a
dream, and *God* brought the dream to fruition. Joseph's assertion
that it was God who sent him to Egypt, not his brothers, does not
excuse their evil actions. He is not baptizing their sin by invoking
God's providential work. On the contrary, Joseph's statement is a

bold affirmation of the power and goodness of God. Not only are God's purposes not thwarted by his brothers' misdeeds, he uses them to accomplish his purposes. The power of God swallows up the sin of Joseph's brothers.

What the Joseph story teaches us about suffering is clear enough. God has the power to work out his purposes even when suffering is all we can see. God may permit sin and suffering in our lives, but his purposes will never be thwarted.

REFLECTIONS

In the illustration that began this chapter, Jodi thinks that everything that happens is part of God's plan. She wants Lisa to embrace leukemia as "God-given," a necessary step in God's foreordained plan. Many Christians treat suffering this way; for them, any discussion of the sovereignty of God goes hand in hand with divine determinism. They assert that God not only knows all but controls all. Every blessing and every curse, every triumph and every failure, every joy and every pain are the work of God, the fulfillment of his plan for creation, even if they remain hopelessly shrouded in mystery to the human eye. That is to say, *everything* that transpires serves the purposes of God. *Nothing* happens outside of God's purposes. Human choice is an illusion.

I would argue that the Bible's depiction of God's sovereignty has a substantially different thrust. It asserts that even in the midst of the worst wickedness, sin and suffering, God is committed to the ultimate good of his children and his creation, and he has the power to work redemptively on their behalf. When Paul says, "We know that all things work together for good for those who love God, who are called according to his purpose" (Rom 8:28), he does not mean that God accomplishes his good purposes by afflicting us with a multitude of sufferings. Rather, he boldly asserts that none of those sufferings is stronger than God. He is strong enough to take what is evil and use it for our good. In the context of Romans 8, it is apparent that this good is primarily understood in terms of salvation, specifically our status as members of the "family of God" (Rom 8:29). No matter how the storm rages, God's purposes for the one who loves him will win out.

It is vital to recognize that when Scripture highlights God's power in action, it does so precisely because God does *not* make everything happen. We are told when God makes a promise, or reveals a purpose, or acts in history, precisely because one cannot deduce that everything that transpires is the work of God. This need not nullify God's power or authority. It simply reveals something of how God uses his power and authority. God's willingness to be genuinely responsive to human choices should already be obvious in light of our discussion in the previous two chapters. Similarly, a survey of the remainder of the biblical approaches to suffering should make it clear that it would be patently false to adduce that all suffering is caused by God and fits into a seamless foreordained plan.

One of the reasons people interpret the sovereignty of God in terms of divine determinism is that they assume a direct correlation between God's knowledge of the future and God's action to make that future occur. Take, for example, a question that I've had more than a few students pose to me over the years: "Did Judas have to betray Jesus to the authorities because Jesus said it would happen?" I am of the mind that Judas chose to betray Jesus. While Scripture consistently confirms that God *knows* all things, there are many reasons to believe that God does not *do* all things. There is a real distinction to be made between knowing the future and making it happen. God is timeless—outside of time. He is past, present and future all at once. As such, he is capable of perceiving the flow of history without dictating it. Certainly God has committed himself to some courses of action. He has made promises and threats. Since he is all-powerful, there is no reason to doubt that he can bring these things to pass. But God can also speak of events that will transpire in the future without having made them happen. Jesus' proclamation to Peter that he will deny him three times is predictive—but the denials are still Peter's to make. God's knowledge that Judas will betray Jesus does not cause him to do so.

As a pastor, professor and friend I have seen violence done to the hurting through misunderstanding the nature of God's sovereignty. This is particularly true when providence is equated with divine determinism. Such an approach runs the risk of alienating the hurting and demonizing God. Must we conclude that it is part of "God's plan" when a young woman is raped, a new father brutally murdered, a child struck down by a drunk driver? Was God working behind the scenes to murder six million Jews in the Holocaust? This approach to God's providence completely misses the mark. It strives to uncover the hand of God where there is only sin. It fails to take into account that even God must reckon with a creation gone awry. Worst of all, it can turn our comforter and healer into our tormenter.

John was driving on a two-lane highway in rural Kansas. His wife, Kate, dozed in the passenger seat at his side, and both kids were nestled into their boosters in the back seat. It had been a wonderful vacation. Three days full of laughter, joy and refreshment. Tomorrow meant a full day of work on a short night's sleep, but John didn't mind. His heart was full. His spirit was content. He hummed to himself as he saw the headlights approaching in the dark night. John's heart leapt in his chest as the headlights swerved directly into his path. Nothing would ever be the same. John lost his entire family to a drunk driver that night. The following months were filled with two forms of torture. On the one hand, John was left to grieve the life he had lost, his children and wife who had been snatched away from him in the blink of an eye. On the other hand, John's theology left him ill equipped to deal with his suffering. His conviction that God's plan can be read into every eventuality left him cold and confused. Instead of receiving comfort from a God that grieves alongside of him and bears his pain, John was left with a God who moves pieces into the right position on a game board—a God whose "plan" involved eliminating John's family because it was the very best way to further his purposes.

I do not doubt that much of how God works in the world may remain shrouded in mystery for us, but it seems both unnecessary and unbiblical to march down the road of divine determinism. At worst, it leaves us with a God who looks much like the devil.

Though we ought to be wary of divine determinism, we cannot lose sight of the fact that God has plans and purposes. When he commits himself to a course of action, there should be no doubt that it will be accomplished—in spite of the obstacles that stand in the way. He is faithful, trustworthy and true to his promises. Joseph seems to grasp this. He is able to recognize the hand of God in the midst of his terrible circumstances because God himself laid the foundation for such an understanding. When Joseph finally attained his position of power in Egypt, he could not help but acknowledge the fulfillment of God's promises and purposes. As he stood before his brothers with the power of life and death in his hands, he could see clearly that he had become the Joseph of his earliest dreams, the sheaf that rises above the other sheaves, the boy who saw the sun and moon and eleven stars bowing before him. If God's plans had come to fruition, how could he not see God's strong hand at work in the journey, taking his trials and bending them to his own purposes? Truly, Joseph's story lay in God's hands. When we choose to place our lives in his sovereign hands, he will guard our stories as well.

5

The Accuser

Suffering and
the Devil

Pine Ridge is the eighth largest Indian reservation in the United States. Many of its inhabitants suffer from chronic poverty, substance abuse and lack of education. Hopelessness runs deep. Nowhere is this more evident than in the soaring rate of suicide among the community's youth. In a recent spate from the end of December 2014 to February 2015, over 100 youths attempted suicide. Children as young as six years old have taken their lives.

One of my students has spent a great deal of time at Pine Ridge. She feels like God is calling her to work for justice, peace and healing on the reservation. She returned from her most recent trip with a disturbing report about an evil spirit. Many of the youth who have survived suicide attempts relate similar stories about conversations with this spirit. In every case, it has calmly and convincingly urged them to consider ending their lives. How is one to make sense of such a malevolent force?

LUKE 22:31-34

> [31] "Simon, Simon, listen! Satan has demanded to sift all of you like wheat, [32] but I have prayed for you that your own faith may not fail; and you, when once you have turned back, strengthen your brothers." [33] And he said to him, "Lord, I am ready to go with you to prison and to death!" [34] Jesus said, "I tell you, Peter, the cock will not crow this day, until you have denied three times that you know me."

Alongside the defining Hebrew confession of belief in one true God, there are regular references to other spiritual entities, the "host of heaven." These angelic forces mediate God's presence as messengers (Gen 18:1-2), protectors (Dan 10:21), representations of God (Gen 32:24-30) and bringers of death and destruction (Ex 12:23). In the book of Job, an important figure appears on the theological landscape for the first time. Known as Satan, which in Hebrew means "the accuser," he presents himself before the Lord alongside the other angels in the first chapter of Job (Job 1:6). His role is to test the commitment of God's servants, to separate out those who simply serve and obey because they reap the rewards of following God from those who love the giver more than the gift. Job's famous troubles begin when the Lord asks Satan to "consider my servant Job" (Job 1:8). In testing Job, Satan inflicts wave after wave of suffering—physical, emotional, social and spiritual. He suits his name well, dogging God to grant him further powers in testing Job. He relishes his running debate with God and is determined to break Job, the model of righteousness. In fact, Satan seems to operate as more than a functionary of God. In their second conversation, God says of Job, "He still persists in integrity, although you incited me against him, to destroy him for no reason" (Job 2:3). Already there is a give and take between the two that makes Satan seem more than a little sinister.

Over time, understanding of Satan's role developed until he was perceived as a full-fledged semi-autonomous enemy of God and his people. By the time of Jesus, the activity of Satan had become a common way of interpreting the suffering of the righteous. Explicitly working counter to the purposes of God, Satan sought to undermine the faith of the righteous, driving them to distraction or despair in the hope of ultimately separating them from God. The accuser plied his trade with the tools at his disposal, principally the propensity of humanity to sin by choosing against God. It was this very disposition that granted Satan a measure of authority. Humanity continued to reject the claims of God's benevolent lordship. On what grounds was God to banish Satan from a world where he had been so explicitly welcomed? The problems of sin and Satan were intertwined. God would have to deal with them both in the same stroke.

This is not to say that Jewish monotheism had given way to a sort of dualism with two equal and opposing forces, God and Satan, locked in combat. Though Satan did not act in obedience to God, it was understood that God, the one true and all-powerful God, remained powerful over Satan. Satan was on God's leash. The leash afforded Satan room to operate destructively within limits, but there was no doubt who was master. In due time, God would put Satan in his place.

In order to understand Luke 22:31-34, we must first take note of four other Lukan passages in which Satan plays a prominent role. The first of these occurs at the very beginning of Jesus' ministry. After his baptism, the Holy Spirit leads Jesus into the wilderness where he is subjected to a series of temptations (Lk 4:1-13). Here we find Satan playing a familiar role. Much like the scenario with Job, God presents him with a righteous man and allows him to test the quality of his faith. The primary parallel, however, is not with Job but with Israel's stubborn wilderness generation, who saw remarkable evidence of God's power and faithfulness and still failed their own series of tests. The parallels are not hard to see. Jesus, like

Israel, finds himself in the wilderness without what he needs to survive. Three times Jesus resists temptation by referring to Deuteronomy, the same book that chronicles Israel's failed tests in the wilderness. He remains in the wilderness for forty days, which parallel the forty years of testing (Deut 8:2-5). *Unlike* the wilderness generation, Jesus emerges from his time of testing successfully. This sets the stage for much of what is to come in Luke. Like Israel, Jesus has had his faith tested (by none other than Satan), but Jesus has demonstrated himself to be the faithful son. The authority he will exercise derives from the fact that he remained wholeheartedly committed to God and his purposes. Satan has no power over him. The narrative ends with a warning to be on the lookout for Satan. His role in the story of Jesus is not over: "When the devil had finished every test, he departed from him until an opportune time" (Lk 4:13).

As Jesus' ministry develops, he extends his authority to those who follow him. In Luke 10:17-20, seventy missionaries return to Jesus with great joy, telling stories of demonic submission. In response Jesus proclaims, "I watched Satan fall from heaven like a flash of lightning" (Lk 10:18). Jesus is declaring the advance of the kingdom of God in the actions of his disciples. Satan will lose his foothold as God's rightful reign is extended. Ultimately, the ministry of Jesus will render Satan impotent.

However, Satan's demise awaits a decisive attack, as the next passage makes clear: "When a strong man, fully armed, guards his castle, his property is safe. But when one stronger than he attacks him and overpowers him, he takes away his armor in which he trusted and divides his plunder" (Lk 11:21-22). The strong man is Satan, and Jesus is the stronger man. The parable portrays the authority of Satan in radical terms. The world has become his castle and though his authority is only temporary, there is little doubt that he exercises dominion. The kingdom of God will not come near as a result of exorcisms alone. They are evidence that God is on the move, but real victory will only be secured when God deals with sin, restoring God's rule over the lives of his people (see Lk 11:24-26). Jesus knows that he must invade Satan's domain and strip away his armor, the power of sin, in order to claim his possessions, people. As the faithful son deals with sin on the cross, Satan's claim on humanity will be made void.

Finally, in Luke 22:3 Satan enters the story once again. The "opportune time" spoken of in 4:13 has arrived. Instead of targeting Jesus, Satan enters into one of his twelve disciples, Judas Iscariot. Thus begins the final drama of the book of Luke, leading up to Jesus' crucifixion and dramatic victory over sin and Satan. But as we will see in Luke 22:31-34, Satan's surgical strike is not limited to Judas but includes all of the disciples.

Luke 22:31-34 is part of Jesus' instruction to his disciples at his last meal. With his passion imminent, Jesus delivers grave news to Peter about what is to unfold. His initial address already has a troubling ring to it: "Simon, Simon, listen!" (Lk 22:31). Peter has not been called Simon since receiving a new name from Jesus in Luke 6:14. Apparently, the new identity that came through relationship with Jesus (Peter means "rock") is in peril.

Jesus tells him that "Satan has demanded to sift all of you like wheat" (Lk 22:31). There is much in this statement to unpack. First, we see that Satan has targeted *all* of the disciples in an attempt to thwart the purposes of God. His aim is precisely what we might expect from the "accuser." He will sift the disciples like wheat, a clear reference to testing. In the face of persecution, suffering and fear, will anything remain of the faith they had in Jesus?

Second, though Satan is clearly working to undermine in the disciples what Jesus has labored to build up, he seems to do so only with permission from God. The relationship implied here is most instructive. Satan "demands" the right to test the disciples in the pattern of Job and the temptations of Jesus in Luke 4. The verb *exaiteō* occurs only here in the New Testament. It can be translated "to ask for" or "to demand." The latter, though perhaps a little bold, is preferable because the verb includes the idea that the one making the request has a right to do so. What is fascinating is that both God and Satan seem compelled to operate within certain constraints. Satan, who seeks to use suffering to separate the disciples from God, must still go to God for permission. For his part, God is compelled to permit the testing of the disciples. It would seem that Satan has the right to see if their faith is genuine. That the stakes are very real is all the more clear when one reflects on the choice of Judas, who has already turned against Jesus at the behest of Satan.

Jesus follows this sobering declaration with words of support: "But I have prayed for you that your own faith may not fail; and you, when once you have turned back, strengthen your brothers" (Lk 22:32). Having described the time of testing that awaits all the disciples, Jesus' focus returns to Peter: "I have prayed for you" (singular). His prayer is that Peter's faith may not fail. That tender shoot of faith that Jesus has spent much of the Gospel of Luke seeking to nurture and grow is about to come under siege. Jesus' prayer is not that Peter's faith will prove to be a match for Satan's tests the way Jesus' own faith was. It is already clear that Jesus anticipates Peter's initial failure ("when once you have turned back"). Rather, his prayer that Peter's faith may not fail is a prayer that *something* of his faith may remain. The verb *ekleipō*, "to fail," refers to the possibility of something "running out." It is used in Luke 16:9 of worldly wealth coming to an end with death. The efficacy of Jesus' prayer will be seen in the ultimate preservation of Peter's faith.

Jesus tells Peter that once he "turns back" he is to strengthen his brothers. He will continue to be a leader for the disciples, a sure "rock" in time of need precisely because Jesus has interceded for him. Within the scope of Luke-Acts, we see this prediction come true, particularly in the Pentecost events detailed in Acts 1:15-26, when Peter boldly proclaims the gospel of Jesus Christ, crucified and resurrected.

Peter is stung by the implication that he will fail Jesus. He objects strenuously, "Lord, I am ready to go with you to prison and to death!" (Lk 22:33). Jesus' reply makes it clear that he could not be more wrong. "I tell you, Peter, the cock will not crow this day, until you have denied three times that you know me" (Lk 22:34). Peter will fall, just like the other disciples. Yet the prophecy contains a word of hope for Peter. Jesus' conversation began by calling Peter "Simon," a reminder of his life before faith, before discipleship, before transformation. Now Jesus calls him "Peter" ("the rock"), the man established in Jesus. There is hope for Peter because Jesus is at work on his behalf from the beginning to the end.

Peter's impending failure points to the fact that the "strong man" of Luke 11:21-22 still has authority. The victory over sin and Satan will be won by Jesus, but he must first go to the cross, submitting to his own final test. On the cross he will bind the strong man and take away his armor, liberating captives like Peter who prove powerless to free themselves—even when they desire to choose the way of faith.

With Jesus' death on the cross, the defeat of Satan is secured. However, those New Testament authors who are reflecting on life after the crucifixion and resurrection continue to see Satan at work in the world. Peter reminds his audience, "Like a roaring lion your adversary the devil prowls around, looking for someone to devour" (1 Pet 5:8). Paul urges forgiveness for the repentant sinner lest the community be "outwitted by Satan; for we are not ignorant of his designs" (2 Cor 2:11). On another occasion, Paul discerns a sinister hand in his thwarted travel plans. "For we wanted to come to you—certainly I, Paul, wanted to again and again—but Satan blocked our way" (1 Thes 2:18).

Though the cross and resurrection have restored peace with God and given the opportunity to revel in his glorious rescue, they have not stripped away the ability to choose against God. Satan continues to tempt and test, leaving suffering and pain, guilt and shame in his wake. Thrashing and flailing in his final death throes before the return of Jesus, Satan continues to take advantage of the lingering presence of sin to separate people from God and wreak havoc against creation.

Reflections

For many modern Western Christians, Satan and demons are merely vestiges of a bygone age. There was a time for this type of thinking in antiquity, the thought goes, but that time has certainly passed. Satan may even be a source of mild embarrassment, something to be explained away.

Three things make me uncomfortable with this conclusion. First, the conflict between God and Satan is clearly a central feature of Jesus' teaching and ministry. Even after Satan's fate is sealed, various books of the New Testament continue to talk about Satan's role and activity in the world.

Second, the trend in the Western intellectual tradition since the Enlightenment has been toward strictly material explanations of reality. From Spinoza to Kant to Bultmann, this has resulted in attempts to demythologize the Christian faith, rewriting the story in a way that is acceptable to modern sensibilities. Much like miracles, there is no room for Satan in this new order.

Yet this is not the perspective of most Christians. Most Christians do not live in Europe or North America, and do not share the same assumptions about what is and is not possible. They don't find the supernatural embarrassing. Quite the contrary, in most of the world the supernatural is an assumed part of life. Perhaps the legacy of the Enlightenment is more mixed than we acknowledge. Maybe the rigorous pursuit of critical understanding opened the door to hubris, and our attempts to define reality have become a way to assert our control. Our situation in the West is reminiscent of the events that followed God's deliverance of his people from Egypt. The Hebrew people grew uncomfortable when Moses met with God on top of Mount Sinai. As the days passed, they sensed their lack of control. They could do nothing but wait, and waiting made them feel powerless. Finally, they encouraged Aaron to fashion an idol for them to represent God, so that they might see him and touch him and control him. I wonder if we have produced a new golden calf so that we might master our reality and avoid the terrible unknown.

Third, my own experience has led me to acknowledge the reality of Satan. I have personally seen, heard, read and experienced enough to know that such encounters are not merely part of a bygone age. One of my favorite C. S. Lewis books is *The Screwtape Letters*. Lewis ingeniously presents us with a series of letters from a high-ranking demon, Screwtape, to his apprentice, Wormwood, concerning effective means of combating the "enemy," God. The preface includes a particularly instructive quote. "There are two equal and opposite errors into which our race can fall about the devils. One is to disbelieve in their existence. The other is to believe, and to feel an excessive and unhealthy interest in them." These two errors apply equally well in considering the role of demonic activity in suffering.

If Satan's primary goal is to separate God from his children, then suffering is one of Satan's greatest tools. It would be a grave error not to look for his "signature" in the personal and communal suffering evident in our world. Time and time again I have encountered students who have turned away from the life of faith because of personal suffering. The death of a friend, divorce of parents, rape, debilitating disease, poverty—I am grieved to see how much pain has been suffered by ones so young. Yet the greatest tragedy is the death of faith. This is Satan's victory, estrangement from God. To disbelieve in the existence of demons is to lose sight of the fact that the suffering we experience is, in some measure, evidence of a spiritual battle between good and evil, God and Satan. If we "flatten" reality we have trouble seeing the whole picture, which includes the activity of the great rebel Satan and his minions. As Jesus says about Satan in the Gospel of John, "The thief comes only to steal and kill and destroy. I came that they may have life, and have it abundantly" (Jn 10:10). Those who live in denial of the thief do so at their own peril.

There is, however, an opposite and equally serious error. It is possible to dwell far too much on Satan's role in suffering, concluding that all suffering represents the work of demonic powers. There are two weighty problems with this approach. First, it diminishes the importance of human agency. The Bible makes it clear that we are responsible for our choices. We are exhorted to choose for God and all that he embodies: faith, hope, love, grace, kindness, gentleness, patience and so on. In the same vein, we are called to reject sin in all of its manifestations; recall the significance of the "two ways" in Hebrew thought. Satan's investment in suffering in no way negates personal responsibility over one's choices. We have freedom to sin and are consequently personally responsible for generating much suffering for ourselves and others.

I saw an example of this approach when I was involved in a church whose ministry to the church body and wider community was flourishing. At one point, a special meeting was called for all members and we were told the shocking news that our pastor, a deeply loved and respected man, had entered into an emotional affair with a congregant. The congregation was understandably distraught. What took me by surprise, however, was the number of people who spoke at that meeting about the work of Satan in our midst. These comments left me feeling conflicted. On the one hand,

I am certain that Satan would like nothing more than to disrupt a community by discrediting its pastor. On the other hand, I couldn't help thinking that it was far too convenient to invoke Satan when confronted with the poor choices of someone we admire—or with our own poor choices, for that matter. The mere fact that repentance and reconciliation (both of which begin with acknowledgment of one's choice to sin) are the first steps toward healing suggests that responsibility does not ultimately fall to Satan.

An undue preoccupation with Satan's role in suffering has another negative consequence: it shifts our focus from God to Satan. We are tempted to think about what Satan is doing rather than what God is doing. We are tempted to spend our time praying against Satan rather than praying to God. Before long we have descended into a full-fledged dualism, with God and Satan positioned as equal combatants. With such a theology it is easy to diagnose all suffering as the work of the enemy. We have sorely missed the mark when Satan takes such a prominent place in our theology. The biblical witness stresses that Satan's power is limited and his defeat has already been secured. He is no equal of God. Furthermore, as noted in the introduction, there are at least eleven other biblical approaches to suffering in the world, making it abundantly clear that it is misguided to detect the hand of Satan in every hardship.

So if God's people are called to take Satan's potential role in suffering seriously without mistakenly assuming that all suffering proceeds from him, we are left with two important questions. First, how do we go about discerning whether Satan is playing a prominent role in our suffering? I wish there was an easy answer to this question (perhaps a little note signed by the devil!). The truth is we must rely on God, who offers his people discernment through the Holy Spirit. In fact, according to 1 Corinthians 12:10, one of the gifts given to particular individuals within the church is "the discernment of spirits." This underscores the notion that discernment should include the larger Christian community. Without divine aid, the workings of the spiritual realm remain shrouded in mystery. Our insight will invariably be limited. More often than not, we must content ourselves with the knowledge that there is more going on than we will ever know.

Second, what are we to do if we discern that demonic opposition is indeed involved in our current situation? We are to resist him with our prayers and our choices while clinging to God, who saves us from our enemies. We must remain mindful of Satan's true purpose, to separate us from God. Additionally, when appropriate, framing one's struggles in terms of "battle" can be freeing and empowering, helping the sufferer move past the haunting "why" of suffering in order to ask "what now?" One of the strengths of the Bible's final book, Revelation, is its ability to help God's people to see clearly the spiritual battle at the heart of their earthly struggles so that they might respond to suffering with courage and conviction.

The New Testament's most basic advice regarding Satan boils down to pursuing God. For example, Ephesians exhorts its audience, "do not make room for the devil" (Eph 4:27). The context makes it clear that choosing for sin provides a foothold for the devil to work. James entreats his audience to "Resist the devil, and he will flee from you. Draw near to God, and he will draw near to you" (Jas 4:7-8). When we choose obedience and faithfulness to God we are doing precisely what we need to do in order to limit the reach of Satan in our lives. We are placing ourselves firmly in God's hands.

No matter what suffering is produced by Satan and his minions, we must never lose sight of the fact that God is bigger. Peter's sifting by Satan led to a threefold denial of Jesus. After these denials, he was a broken man. Yet that was not the end of his story. Victory belonged to God, who restored him to fellowship. No matter what suffering Satan might inflict or how one might have succumbed to his power, hope remains in God.

6

I Am

The Mystery of Suffering

✝

I like answers. In a way, understanding something and being able to explain it makes it real to me. My education, of course, validated this disposition. I was encouraged to solve problems, assess evidence, and draw critical conclusions. Not surprisingly, much of my early growth as a Christian involved investigating Scripture, building a systematic theology, and gleaning insights from other Christians, both historical and contemporary. My efforts were certainly rewarded with deeper understanding. However, some things failed to yield their secrets in spite of my closest scrutiny. At the time, I found these mysteries unsettling. Honestly, I think I distrusted the truthfulness of something that eluded my explanation and categorization. I see now that this distrust was actually rooted in loss of control. Slowly but surely I have come to see that if God is really and truly beyond me, then it is only reasonable that there would be mysteries too deep and wide for me. Ultimately, God does not call me to trust in *my* understanding of him; he calls me to trust *him*.

Job 40:8-14

> [8] Will you even put me in the wrong?
>   Will you condemn me that you may be justified?
> [9] Have you an arm like God,
>   and can you thunder with a voice like his?
> [10] "Deck yourself with majesty and dignity;
>   clothe yourself with glory and splendor.
> [11] Pour out the overflowings of your anger,
>   and look on all who are proud, and abase them.
> [12] Look on all who are proud, and bring them low;
>   tread down the wicked where they stand.
> [13] Hide them all in the dust together;
>   bind their faces in the world below.
> [14] Then I will also acknowledge to you
>   that your own right hand can give you victory.

The trials of Job are well known. This righteous man lost his property and his children in a single day. His body was afflicted with painful sores. His own wife urged him to curse God and die. The consolation of friends turned to rebuke as they sought a reason for Job's horrible situation. Desiring to free him from further pain and suffering, they urged him to confess his sin to God.

The beginning and ending of the book of Job give the reader insight into the cause of Job's suffering. In the first chapters, Satan asserts that the blessings of God are responsible for the development of Job's righteousness. By the end of the book, once Job's righteousness has been established as independent of God's blessing, God once again blesses Job. But Job knows of none of this. It is not even revealed to him at the end of the book.

As far as Job was concerned, his suffering was without purpose or meaning. In the midst of his trials, Job famously proved unwilling to forsake his innocence. It was, after all, the only thing that remained to him. He cried out to God for vindication and deliverance, but without answer. In due time, his cries turned to accusations. If Job was innocent, then God must be guilty. *He* was responsible for this endless suffering, and as far as Job was concerned it rendered God's justice impotent.

As surely as God lives, who has denied me justice,
    the Almighty, who has made me taste bitterness of soul,
as long as I have life within me,
    the breath of God in my nostrils,
my lips will not speak wickedness,
    and my tongue will utter no deceit.
I will never admit you are in the right;
    till I die, I will not deny my integrity.
I will maintain my righteousness and never let go of it;
    my conscience will not reproach me as long as I live.
    (Job 27:2-6 NIV 1984)

In chapter 38, Job receives an answer, though perhaps not the kind of answer he anticipated. God addresses Job out of the whirlwind. Job's rant comes to an end as God takes the role of questioner: "Who is this that darkens counsel by words without knowledge? Gird up your loins like a man, I will question you, and you shall declare to me" (Job 38:2-3). God proceeds to lay before Job all the wondrous marvels of creation. Both great and small, they reflect the power and knowledge of the maker. Job's response to this magnificent tour of God's creative work is to commit himself to silence, but clearly this response is not adequate. God is looking for something more; his second challenge begins with the very words of the first challenge: "Gird up your loins like a man; I will question you, and you declare to me" (40:7).

This second challenge begins with our passage and concludes with a meditation on two of God's more fearsome creations, Behemoth and Leviathan, each of which expresses something of the uncontrollable power and amazing scope of God's creation. Job, who has stood in the role of accuser, must now defend his position in the light of new evidence. The NIV reproduces the Hebrew more literally in verse 8 than the NRSV, providing insight into what is at stake. "Would you discredit my justice? Would you condemn me to justify yourself?" (40:8). Job and his friends have all been operating under a false either/or premise. Either Job is a sinner whose suffering is the justice of God at work (the position of Job's friends), or God has abrogated his justice and has done Job harm in spite of Job's innocence (Job's position). It is important to note that God has not accused Job of sin. Rather, God objects to the assertion of Job's innocence at the expense of his own justice. Job is right about his innocence, but he is grievously mistaken to think that it compromises the justice of God.

God continues, "Have you an arm like God, and can you thunder with a voice like his?" (40:9). Is Job God's equal? Can he do what God does or know what God knows? Is he in a position to know the mind of God or his purposes? If Job thinks that the administration of justice is a simple matter, then he should take it upon himself. "Deck yourself with majesty and dignity; clothe yourself with glory and splendor" (40:10). Assume the royal role, Job! Play regent over creation and administer justice as you see fit. "Pour out the overflowings of your anger, and look on all who are proud, and abase them. Look on all who are proud, and bring them low; tread down the wicked where they stand. Hide them all in the dust together; bind their faces in the world below" (40:11-13). If you can do all of this, says God, "then I myself will admit to you that your own right hand can save you" (40:14 NIV). How can Job respond to such a prompting? Obviously he lacks the power and authority to administer such justice. He cannot abase the proud and hide the wicked in the dust. He doesn't have an "arm like God" or a "voice that thunders like his." Nor does Job have the wisdom and knowledge of

God. Would Job know who the proud are that need to be brought low? Would he discern who the wicked are so that he might judge them? Would there be room for repentance, mercy, grace and transformation? Would Job, the righteous judge, have destroyed himself when his own demand for vindication caused him to point the finger at God in condemnation, a display of pride if there ever was one?

God's challenge makes it clear that Job is small, powerless and exceptionally limited—but not without a voice. This is the voice that called God out of hiding. This is the voice that has earned the right to hear God's reply. It is only because Job truly understands something of God's justice that he raises his complaint to God. In this sense, he is very different from the rest of creation; he is made in the very image of God, and God honors him as such. Nevertheless, this understanding does not make him God. Just as there is a profound difference between the power and understanding of humanity and the created order (over which humanity is granted dominion), so too there is a profound difference between God and humanity (over whom God has dominion). It is this difference that God is pressing home upon Job. Though uniquely capable of knowing God, Job could never be God.

What both meditations on the created order are supposed to impress upon Job is that the justice of God lies beyond him. He lacks both the power and the understanding to lay hold of it. God's creation of the world in all its magnificence represents an act of power that lies infinitely beyond Job. Moreover, the very nature of the world as God created it defies Job's understanding. God granted his creation freedom. He tolerates its danger. He delights in the Behemoth and the Leviathan, "which I made just as I made you" (40:15). If God's creation remains a mystery to Job, so will God's governance. He is in no place to evaluate the justice of God.

What kind of answer is this to Job's plight? Above all, it is an answer of presence. It is significant that God spoke to Job out of the whirlwind. God's justice may remain beyond Job's comprehension, but his presence makes all the difference. As Job will say, "I had heard of you by the hearing of the ear, but now my eyes see you" (42:5). In other words, Job's perspective has been changed by an interaction with the living God, leading him to recant his accusations (42:6).

This is not a declaration of God's providential action in history. There is no sense that Job will be able to look back on the events of his life and discern the reason behind his suffering. God explicitly avoids providing Job with such a reason. It is enough for Job to know that God is God and he is not.

REFLECTIONS

This approach to suffering emphasizes the great distance between us and God in order to remind us that the suffering we experience might always remain a mystery. It cautions us never to become dogmatic in our interpretations of suffering. Our desire to comprehend the suffering in our lives, like every other aspect of life, must be approached with open hands, in humility, fully aware that only the great I Am sees all things, understands all things and can do all things.

The mystery that continues to shroud some suffering is not without its advantages. When faced with mystery, there is nothing left to do but go to God, releasing our burdens, our pains and our very selves into the hands of the Almighty. Whether we lift our voices to the heavens in grief or bow our heads in peaceful submission, we openly acknowledge that he is God and we are not. It is simultaneously an admission of our finitude and a declaration of God's magnitude. Sometimes there is nothing left but to stand before him and know his greatness—a greatness capable of swallowing up any pain or hurt or grief.

After several years of marriage, my wife, Julie, and I desired to start a family. Like many couples in our situation, we never anticipated having trouble conceiving. After months of unsuccessful attempts, we agreed to have some tests done. They revealed that it was virtually impossible for us to conceive without medical assistance—specifically in vitro fertilization. As the end of a second unsuccessful cycle of in vitro loomed, we decided to move toward adoption. We felt like God had prepared our hearts for this new adventure, and we eagerly threw ourselves into the process. We were excited to begin our family. When the doctor called to give us the news about our final set of embryos, we were completely caught off guard. We were pregnant! We were absolutely elated, celebrating God's answer to our prayers. We were also a little confused, having emotionally made the transition toward adoption.

We celebrated with our community, with all those who had prayed for us and hoped for us in the long journey of infertility. We laid plans and prepared for the arrival of our baby, delighting in each positive checkup at the doctor's office.

Then came the blow. Our little miracle had died sometime at the end of the first trimester. The heartbeat was gone. The fragile life within my wife's womb had been snuffed out. We were overwhelmed with grief. Our hearts ached for the baby we would never hold, never kiss, never know. The world seemed to grow pale and cold. Our hopes and dreams, so recently kindled into a blazing fire, now offered only the most meager warmth.

But the grief did not come alone. It was accompanied by confusion. Why had we become pregnant? Why had the baby died? Why had God taken us through this if we were meant to adopt all along? The questions multiplied, but no answers were forthcoming—save one. God answered us with his presence. He heard every expression of grief. He watched the flood of tears. He held us in our utter brokenness. For our part, we surrendered to him. We offered ourselves to the one who holds all things together—and it was enough. In fact, our grief was oddly fuller, richer and somehow more sufficient because we didn't understand. Perhaps "answers" would have gotten in the way. In the days after our baby died, Julie and I both penned letters to our baby. Mine read like this.

Dear Baby,

It is hard to say goodbye . . . for it is a goodbye to so many things. It is a goodbye to the face I won't see, a goodbye to the laughter I will never hear, a goodbye to the child I will never hold. But it is more than that. Saying goodbye to you means saying goodbye to a future that will never happen for Julie and me. It is letting go of one dream so that we can receive God's good plans for us with open hands and hearts.

Perhaps we will meet again and we will look into each other's eyes in the world to come and we will have the blessing not only of "what is"—but every "what could have been."

This is my hope. This is my prayer to our father. I thank you for your brief visit with us. It kindled within me joy and pleasure that can only come from God. And so, you must have been a gift from him to us, a love gained and a pain suffered. Know that I loved you and if you would have remained with us, my love for you would have flourished. Find peace and joy with Jesus. And so I say goodbye.

Love,
Your Papa

Our journey, of course, was far from over. As one chapter of our lives closed, God opened up another. When we adopted our first child from Korea, any lingering fears were immediately purged by our unbridled joy. At four months old, she welcomed *us* home with coos and smiles. We named her Eliana, "God has answered."

God Wins

Suffering and the Future

One of the great crises in Jewish history unfolded in the 160s BC under the Seleucid King Antiochus IV. Angered by the rebellious nature of his Jewish subjects and the mistreatment of his chosen representative in Jerusalem, Antiochus IV committed himself to stamping out Judaism. He outlawed traditional Jewish practices and ordered that sacrifices be made to Zeus. The very existence of Judaism seemingly hung by a thread. Many Jews were tortured and killed when they refused to abide by the new laws. The books of 1 and 2 Maccabees tell the story of these martyrdoms and the ensuing revolt, which led to the preservation of the Jewish people. One chapter, 2 Maccabees 7, narrates the gruesome death of seven brothers and their mother. One at a time, these brothers' hands, feet, scalp and tongue were cut off because they would not eat the required swine flesh. After this torture, the still-living victim was taken to burning hot cauldrons to be burned to death. After each death, the poor mother would gather her sons and encourage them to stay faithful to the end.

What gave these martyrs the strength to stand up to such persecution? The answer can be found in the final testimony of the brothers themselves. Each clung to the belief that God's justice extends beyond the present life. For example, one brother boldly said to the king, "One cannot but choose to die at the hands of mortals and to cherish the hope God gives of being raised again by him. But for you there will be no resurrection to life!" (2 Macc 7:14). Another, when his time had come, stretched forth his hands and said, "I got these from Heaven, and because of his laws I disdain them, and from him I hope to get them back again" (2 Macc 7:11). A hope strong enough to see one through such devilish torture is potent indeed. But where does such hope come from?

ROMANS 8:18-25

> [18] I consider that the sufferings of this present time are not worth comparing with the glory about to be revealed to us. [19] For the creation waits with eager longing for the revealing of the children of God; [20] for the creation was subjected to futility, not of its own will but by the will of the one who subjected it, in hope [21] that the creation itself will be set free from its bondage to decay and will obtain the freedom of the glory of the children of God. [22] We know that the whole creation has been groaning in labor pains until now; [23] and not only the creation, but we ourselves, who have the first fruits of the Spirit, groan inwardly while we wait for adoption, the redemption of our bodies. [24] For in hope we were saved. Now hope that is seen is not hope. For who hopes for what is seen? [25] But if we hope for what we do not see, we wait for it with patience.

Every one of us has a story—a past that shaped us, a present that confronts us with new defining choices and a future waiting to be discovered. Like it or not, suffering invariably plays a role in these stories. Sometimes it threatens to define the story, turning it into a tragedy. It can strip away choices, stomp out dreams and even bring the story to a woeful conclusion.

The wicked are not the only ones who suffer. God's people have learned the hard way that suffering can result even in the death of the righteous. As in the case of the martyrs mentioned above, how is one to understand the story of a faithful person who dies a martyr's death? Who has the final word in our story?

Eschatology provides an answer to these questions. Eschatology is the study of the "last things," the resolution of God's story in the world. Eschatology encourages us to see that our individual stories are just a small part of God's great story. God's story also has a past, present and future. However, unlike ours, his story spans creation and covenants, Israel and the church. Eschatology asserts that God will dramatically intervene in the course of history in order to achieve his own good purposes. Hence, eschatology is historical in nature; it deals with events that will happen in the course of real time. Though it affirms an eternal destiny for individuals, it does not focus much on life immediately after death (which shifts the primary focus back to the individual's story). Rather, it asserts that God's story as it plays out in history is the defining story. Every other story finds its true meaning in this grand narrative.

Eschatology seeks to transform God's people in three ways. First, it opens our eyes to see our story within the context of God's story. Each of us lives and breathes in a single moment of his grand story— no more, no less. In order to make sense of suffering, we must consider the whole sweep of the story. Second, it encourages God's people to apprehend their importance in this larger story. The moment we occupy and the way we respond in the midst of it have lasting implications for the story, even though we may not be able to see in the moment of crisis how our suffering furthers the story of God. Third, and most of all, it aims to tell where God's story is going. God will win in the great drama of history. Eschatology is, at its heart, the proclamation that God will have victory over Satan and sin, suffering and death. He will intervene decisively to set things right, to restore justice and to deliver his people from bondage, both earthly and spiritual. The culmination of God's story includes all of his people, past and present. God's victory will mean new life for those who have walked in faith and died.

The great majority of Jews living prior to Jesus thought eschato-logically. They expected God to intervene dramatically within history to conquer Satan and sin, suffering and death. It was un-imaginable that these realities would continue to define God's story. God's goodness, God's power, God's covenant faithfulness, God's commitment to his creation—all of these demanded that God triumph over evil. While the stories faithful Jews told each other about God's impending victory often disagreed about details of the story's resolution, there were several general features they shared.

First, death would be overcome. Generally this was conceived in terms of a general resurrection. God would give new bodies to the living and the dead. Second, God's justice would be made plain for all to see. There would be a final judgment—a separation of the righteous from the wicked. The righteous would be vindicated, and the wicked would experience the wrath of God. Third, God's promises would be fulfilled. Israel would be restored to a position of honor before God. The long-hoped-for Davidic ruler would once again sit on the throne. Sin, the ever-lurking enemy of God's people, would be done away with once and for all. Finally, God's victory would bring all of creation full circle. It would be like a return to paradise, a time before sin, death, suffering and the dominion of Satan. Creation itself would be restored to its initial splendor. Figure 7.1 represents the prevailing Jewish eschatological per-spective prior to Jesus.

When Jesus came on the scene, he came preaching an eschato-logical message. He urged his listeners to pay special attention to the unique moment they occupied in history, a moment when God was indeed dramatically intervening to claim victory over darkness.

Figure 7.1

Both his preaching and his ministry trumpeted the eschatological action of God. "The time is fulfilled, and the kingdom of God has come near; repent and believe in the good news" (Mk 1:15). In the person and ministry of Jesus, the long-awaited Christ, the last things had drawn near. Healings and exorcisms followed in his wake, tangible signs of God's impending victory over suffering and death. He offered fellowship with God and participation in his kingdom, the opportunity to become sons and daughters of the King, so that they might share in the glory that God intended for his people. He demanded uncompromising allegiance, denial of self and love of enemy. He threatened the old order, proclaiming the birth of a new age. In his flesh he made a new covenant that breathed life into old prophetic longings: "I will give them one heart, and put a new spirit within them; I will remove the heart of stone from their flesh and give them a heart of flesh, so that they may follow my statutes and keep my ordinances and obey them. Then they shall be my people, and I will be their God" (Ezek 11:19-20). With his death he ransomed humanity from sin, defeating the powers of darkness. In his resurrection lay the promise of new life and a new way of living. In Jesus, the eschatological moment had arrived. God's final victory had begun—but it had only begun.

In Jesus, Jewish expectations about the resolution of God's story were both fulfilled and turned upside down. God had triumphed

over sin, but sin remained in the world. Jesus' resurrection proclaimed God's victory over death, but death continued to claim the
lives of both the righteous and the wicked. Jesus took his place as
God's true Messiah, heir of the Davidic throne and redeemer of
Israel, fulfillment of God's promises. Nevertheless, many within
Israel spurned Jesus the King. Jesus opened up the possibility of a
new life with God, a life lived in the power of his Spirit. Yet those
who lived by his Spirit found themselves embattled and persecuted.

The climactic chapter in God's story had indeed begun in the
eschatological event of Jesus' life, death and resurrection. The
course of the story was irrevocably changed by God's direct intervention. The consummation of all things could now be glimpsed on
the horizon, tantalizingly close and so obviously real. In fact, the
people of God already experienced it in part. Evidence of new life
abounded. The people of God became his new temple, with the
Holy Spirit empowering them to live new lives under a new covenant. Previous boundaries fell away as the power of God's future
flooded the present. Both the marginalized and the foreigner were
welcomed into God's new community, a tangible sign of God
bringing all things under his Lordship.

However, this climactic chapter would come to an end only with
a *second* eschatological event, the earthly return of the risen Lord.
With this second coming, the fullness of the "new age" will be revealed. Resurrection of the dead, final judgment and the renewal of
creation all await Jesus' return. The eschatological expectations of
Jesus' Jewish contemporaries had been accurate in many ways, but
the picture was more complex than they had imagined. This can be
seen from figure 7.2.

Our passage, Romans 8:18-25, seeks to understand present suffering in light of God's story, especially the wonderful future that
awaits those who have joined their lives with Christ. As a whole,
Romans 8 is a triumphant declaration of the benefits of Christ for

all those who will receive them. Paul begins the chapter with an extended discussion of the Spirit who dwells within all those who are in Christ Jesus (Rom 8:1-13). This in turn leads to a second benefit: "All who are led by the Spirit are children of God" (Rom 8:14). A new status is bestowed on those who follow Jesus. They are children of God, having "received a spirit of adoption" (Rom 8:15). As adopted sons and daughters of the Father, they are also heirs: "Heirs of God and joint heirs with Christ—if, in fact, we suffer with him so that we may also be glorified with him" (Rom 8:17). The path to sonship/daughtership is intimately connected with Jesus. His obedience in the face of suffering must become our own, so that we too might have a share in the glorious conclusion of the story as heirs of God and joint heirs with Christ.

	1st Eschatological Moment *Jesus' Life, Death and Resurrection*	2nd Eschatological Moment *Jesus' Second Coming*
Flow of History		
Effects of the Fall *Sin, Death, Suffering* The "Old Age"	Already and Not Yet *God's Kingdom Has Come,* *But Not Yet in Its Fullness*	New Creation No Sin, Death, Suffering The "New Age"

Figure 7.2

Verse 18 puts this suffering into perspective: "I consider that the sufferings of this present time are not worth comparing with the glory about to be revealed to us" (Rom 8:18). We get a further glimpse into the "suffering of this present time" in Romans 8:35, when Paul speaks of "hardship, or distress, or persecution, or famine, or nakedness, or peril, or sword." Such suffering can be endured because it pales in comparison with the glory that will be revealed to the children of God. This glory outstrips anything we can possibly imagine. We will partake in the very glory of God, the same glory that he extended to his faithful son Jesus. This is what it means to be heirs of God and joint heirs with Christ.

Paul then makes it clear that those who suffer for the sake of Christ are not the only ones who have their eyes fixed on the future: "For the creation waits with eager longing for the revealing of the children of God" (Rom 8:19). The creation itself waits for God to bring to fruition what he initiated in the death and resurrection of his Son. The entire cosmos has a stake in what God is doing, and it waits with bated breath. Paul lays special emphasis on the anticipation of creation; the verse literally reads, "For the eager expectation (*apokaradokia*) of creation eagerly awaits (*apekdechetai*) the revelation of the children of God."

At first glance, Paul's reference to a future "revealing of the children of God" might seem odd given his previous assertions about the benefits extended to those who currently find themselves "in Christ," including the benefit of adoption into his family. In reality, it is entirely in keeping with Pauline eschatology. In light of the twin eschatological events of Jesus' death and resurrection, on the one hand, and his future return on the other, life is lived within the tension of the "already" and the "not yet." In one sense, the death and resurrection of Jesus have *already* resulted in innumerable benefits, including adoption into God's family and salvation. These things are as certain as the character and intention of God, and the Spirit testifies to their reality (Rom 8:16). Nevertheless, they are promises awaiting final consummation. Only when Jesus returns to judge the living and the dead will salvation be experienced and the children of God revealed. This is the historical moment for which creation longs.

As Paul continues, we see that the fate of creation is entwined with that of humanity: "For the creation was subjected to futility, not of its own will but by the will of the one who subjected it, in hope that the creation itself will be set free from its bondage to decay and will obtain the freedom of the glory of the children of God" (Rom 8:20-21). God determined that this would be the case so that the redemption of humanity might usher in the renewal of creation itself. Surely the consequences of the fall are in view here: "Cursed is the ground because of you; in toil you shall eat of it all the days of your life; thorns and thistles it shall bring forth for you" (Gen 3:17-18). Just as humanity's sin brought disorder and death to the whole cosmos, so the final victory of God will mean cosmic renewal. This is more than a return to paradise; it will be the birth of a "new creation." In the words of Isaiah, "I am about to create new heavens and a new earth; the former things shall not be remembered or come to mind" (Is 65:17). The transformation awaiting creation is a movement from a state of slavery to a state of freedom. The reception of the glory that awaits the children of God will signal freedom and renewal for all creation.

In the next verses, Paul provides a new image to describe the eager longing of creation. "We know that the whole creation has been groaning in labor pains until now; and not only creation, but we ourselves, who have the first fruits of the Spirit, groan inwardly while we wait for adoption, the redemption of our bodies" (Rom 8:22-23). Labor pains are an exceedingly common image in Jewish eschatology (including the preaching of Jesus). On the one hand, they indicate the nearness of the end, the joyful conclusion of a pregnancy that results in new life. On the other hand, they point to the difficulty of the last hours, the trial that inevitably precedes the longed-for birth. Many Jewish eschatological scenarios suggest that suffering increases as the moment of God's intervention draws nigh. These "tribulations" test the faithfulness of God's people at the conclusion of the old age and move the world quickly toward the judgment of God. According to Paul, the death and resurrection of Jesus set the wheels in motion. They were the beginning of the labor pains, which signaled that the time of birthing was at hand.

Creation's groaning is matched by our own, the groaning of those "who have the first fruits of the Spirit." The first gleanings of the field were taken to the temple and offered to God in thanksgiving for the harvest. They were a cause of celebration precisely because the rest of the harvest lay out in the fields, ready for reaping. That which had been sown in hope had taken root and grown. It had received the water and nutrients it needed to thrive. It had not been ravaged by wind, storm, frost or drought. The harvest was at hand, as tangibly present as the temple itself, a reminder of God's goodness and faithfulness in an uncertain world. Similarly, Paul asserts that those who belong to Christ have the first fruits of the Spirit. God's longed-for intervention in history is hypothesis no more. It is no longer mere expectation encapsulated in eschatological scenarios. No, God has already acted to save humanity. The first fruits of this great harvest are already present in the person of the Spirit, a gift of God to all those found in his son. The Spirit is proof of what is to come, a reminder that the rest of the harvest is at hand. The birthing process is underway. The fullness of the new age is about be revealed.

Verse 19 described creation's eager expectation for the "revealing of the sons of God." Verse 23 reinforces this idea. The groaning, the labor pains, the first fruits of the harvest—each of these communicates anticipation of the same future. "We wait for adoption, the redemption of our bodies." We wait for Jesus' return. We already live in the reality of God's promise ("You have received a spirit of adoption," Rom 8:15), but we long for the day when we will know even as we are known, when our membership in God's family is proclaimed from the heavens. In like manner, Jesus' resurrection is a potent reminder of God's promise to redeem his people from death, but we still groan for the day when we will receive our own resurrection bodies.

Paul concludes our passage with a brief statement reinforcing the future dimension of our faith in Christ. "For in hope we were saved. Now hope that is seen is not hope. For who hopes for what is seen? But if we hope for what we do not see, we wait for it with patience" (Rom 8:24-25). No matter how much we have already received from Christ's death and resurrection, no matter how wonderful the benefits, the Christian life is still a life of hope. This hope is not wishful thinking or theological conjecture. It is fueled by the presence of labor pains and first fruits, tangible evidence of what is coming. Nevertheless, it remains in the future, and cannot be "seen." Thus the believer, like creation, groans for the return of Christ, the completion of the work initiated in his death and resurrection. If our sufferings are to be endured in light of this glorious conclusion, then we have no choice but to wait for it. But this is no passive waiting. The Greek literally reads, "through patience we eagerly expect" (*di hypomonēs apekdechometha*). In this context, patience is much closer to perseverance. The children of God are called to steadfastly maintain a heightened sense of expectation. Their longing for the future should be cultivated, not subdued, for it enables them to cope with the trials and tribulations of the present. If we have indeed given ourselves to Christ, then his story has become our own. We joyfully participate in his kingdom work, knowing with certainty that the time is coming when the power of Satan and sin, suffering and death will be done away with once and for all.

REFLECTIONS

Eschatology's strength as a means of confronting suffering lies in its ability to breathe hope and comfort into the darkest circumstances. Eschatology affirms that there is a future we cannot currently glimpse, a fitting resolution to the story of God. It is no small comfort to know that God will have the last word in our lives and in human history. Every wrong will be made right, every suffering redeemed. The future is life and wholeness and glory. Eschatology fuels our imagination, helping us to accept the most brutal circumstances because we know what the future holds. The pain of today will pass into the sweetness of tomorrow.

Romans 8 also looks backward, reminding us that creation itself has suffered the effects of humanity's sin. Perhaps this helps us understand the destructive power unleashed by nature. It is all part of a world sundered from the original purposes of God. Chaos and rebellion are made manifest in the wind, the waves and the earth.

Alzheimer's disease defined the last years of my grandmother's life. Slowly but surely, she faded away. A brilliant woman who once spoke nine languages, she struggled to find words to express herself. At the end, she could no longer feed herself, clothe herself or recognize her loved ones. She was a shell of the woman she had once been. Her quick wit and bright eyes were gone. Her mind had been stolen away. Worst of all, the disease took over a decade to do its damage. For most of that time my grandmother had some sense of what was happening to her. She was filled with anxiety and despair over losing herself. How does one cope with this sort of "unbecoming"? Where does one turn for hope? In such moments it is a great comfort to remember that even as the future belongs to God, so do we. God has revealed his plans for humanity in Jesus. My grandmother will "become" again. Through the power of God she will be resurrected—restored, body and mind. As the psalmist says, "You have turned my mourning into dancing; you have taken off my sackcloth and clothed me with joy, so that my soul may praise you and not be silent. O Lord my God, I will give thanks to you forever" (Ps 30:11-12).

As a response to suffering, focusing on eschatology has its shortcomings. First, it is much more a response to suffering than an explanation of it. Those who lean on it in times of difficulty and despair must look elsewhere in order to discern *why* their particular suffering has transpired. Eschatology affirms that the world is not yet as it should be, or as it will be. Just as Satan, sin and death continue to play a role in this present age, so too suffering is part of life in our fallen world, which waits with eager longing for the revealing of the children of God.

Second, a focus on eschatology could inadvertently mute God's intention for his people to be agents of change in the world. Dwelling singularly on the hopes and dreams of a future age could result in a passive resignation to evil in the present. One example of a refusal to do so is the civil rights movement. African American churches were the seedbed for this cultural revolution, but the movement that emerged in response to their suffering was by no means inevitable. These churches could have shirked their calling as agents of social advancement and instead spent their time urging patient endurance in light of eschatological reward. But they did not just pray "your kingdom come." They participated in its coming, bearing witness to the transformation set in motion by Jesus' death and resurrection, the penetration of God's new age into the old.

Ultimately, eschatology fuels hope, enabling it to burn brightly in this present age. If we have a glorious future in God, then the present is the beginning of eternity. What we do matters! In fact, it may have eternal significance. We are free to pursue the aims of the kingdom with abandon, knowing that no peril, obstacle or hardship we might face is bigger than God. "For I am convinced that neither death, nor life, nor angels, nor rulers, nor things present, nor things to come, nor powers, nor height, nor depth, nor anything else in all creation, will be able to separate us from the love of God in Christ Jesus our Lord" (Rom 8:38-39).

8

Running the Race

Suffering as Training

Around six o'clock in the evening on April 4, 1968, Martin Luther King Jr. stepped onto the balcony outside room 306 of the Lorraine Motel in Memphis. As he exchanged words with some friends in the parking lot below him, he was gunned down in cold blood. As the chief voice of the civil rights movement, King had been the object of numerous threats. Many of those threats had already resulted in acts of violence. His house was bombed. He had a knife plunged into his chest. Each one seemed to strengthen his resolve. He knew that his fight for justice might lead to his death, but he seemed prepared for it. In the last sermon he preached, King said,

> Well, I don't know what will happen now. We've got some difficult days ahead. But it doesn't really matter with me now, because I've been to the mountaintop. And I don't mind. Like anybody, I would like to live a long life. Longevity has its place. But I'm not concerned about that now. I just want to do God's will. And He's allowed me to go up to the mountain. And I've looked over. And I've seen the Promised Land. I may not get there with you. But I want you to know tonight, that we, as a people, will get to the Promised Land!

How was Dr. King able to maintain his focus and commitment when faced with his own death? How had he developed the courage necessary to press on?

HEBREWS 12:1-13

[1] Therefore, since we are surrounded by so great a cloud of witnesses, let us also lay aside every weight and the sin that clings so closely, and let us run with perseverance the race that is set before us, [2] looking to Jesus the pioneer and perfecter of our faith, who for the sake of the joy that was set before him endured the cross, disregarding its shame, and has taken his seat at the right hand of the throne of God. [3] Consider him who endured such hostility against himself from sinners, so that you may not grow weary or lose heart. [4] In your struggle against sin you have not yet resisted to the point of shedding your blood. [5] And you have forgotten the exhortation that addresses you as children—

"My child, do not regard lightly the discipline of the Lord,
    or lose heart when you are punished by him;
[6] for the Lord disciplines those whom he loves,
    and chastises every child whom he accepts."

[7] Endure trials for the sake of discipline. God is treating you as children; for what child is there whom a parent does not discipline? [8] If you do not have that discipline in which all children share, then you are illegitimate and not his children. [9] Moreover, we had human parents to discipline us, and we respected them. Should we not be even more willing to be subject to the Father of spirits and live? [10] For they disciplined us for a short time as seemed best to them, but he disciplines us for our good, in order that we may share his holiness. [11] Now, discipline always seems painful rather than pleasant at the time, but later it yields the peaceful fruit of righteousness to those who have been trained by it. [12] Therefore lift your drooping hands and strengthen your weak knees, [13] and make straight paths for your feet, so that what is lame may not be put out of joint, but rather be healed.

Hebrews is a sermon addressed to a people who know suffering well. The author assures them that their suffering is not a sign of the Lord's displeasure. In fact, the opposite is true. Their suffering reveals that God cares for them. All of his children can expect to encounter difficulty and hardship. He will even use this suffering for their good. It is one of the means by which he instructs those that he loves, growing them into maturity. Trust, obedience, endurance, hope and ultimately Christlikeness—God cultivates all these through the fire of adversity.

Hebrews 11 presents a long list of those who demonstrated faith in God. Generation after generation of the faithful are listed, marked out by their obedience to God in spite of various challenges. This "cloud of witnesses" becomes the basis of the sermon's exhortation in the beginning of the next chapter. Hebrews 12:1-13 weaves together two analogies that seek to transform the community's perception of suffering. Verses 1-4 and 11-12 portray the life of discipleship in terms of a race. Success in this race depends on endurance and effective training, which involve suffering. Verses 5-10 move into a different analogy: though all children are instructed by their parents, such instruction is rarely pleasant. Rather, genuine growth generally lies on the far side of hardship, pain and challenge. Together, these two analogies emphasize God's use of suffering to instruct and form those he loves.

"Let us also lay aside every weight and the sin that clings so closely, and let us run with perseverance the race that is set before us" (Heb 12:1). This race of faith is not one that we run against others. Rather, victory in the race means the triumph of the "true self" over against all of the lesser possibilities for our lives. Victory is to be found in God, conformed to the image of his Son in such a way that affirms and honors our own uniqueness. If we have learned anything from the cloud of witnesses it is that winning the race will take everything we have. It will entail struggle and hardship, difficult choices and perseverance. In part, success is determined by our willingness and ability to throw off those things that would hinder our running, "every weight and sin." The chances of crossing the finish line are slim for those who try to run the race laden with extra baggage. Part of our training thus means being weaned from such things, whether they are explicitly harmful, like sin, or simply impediments to running the race effectively. We must also train in order to cultivate the necessary "perseverance" or "endurance" (*hypomonē*). The verbal form of this same term (*hypomenō*) appears at critical junctures throughout the following verses (Heb 12:2, 3, 7), highlighting its importance to the flow of the argument.

The final and greatest example of faith in the cloud of witnesses is Jesus, the "pioneer and perfecter of our faith." (Heb 12:2). As pioneer, Jesus blazes the trail we are to follow. He is the ultimate example of faith, the truly faithful Son who shows us how to live in obedience to the Father. Significantly, Jesus' faith led him straight to the cross. Jesus, like the audience of Hebrews, knew suffering. He too was called to "endure." Yet Jesus knew that there was more to suffering than meets the eye. He knew that his submission to the cross would open up the door to joy. Because of his obedience to the Father, he "has taken his seat at the right hand of the throne of God" (Heb 12:2). But Jesus is not only the pioneer; he is also the perfecter of our faith. He is the one that makes the goal of our faith, life with God, possible. Jesus shows us how the race set before us is run and makes it possible for us to run it.

A look back through the sermon reveals that the groundwork for these twin roles had been laid earlier. Two references in particular indicate the importance of suffering to Jesus' roles as pioneer and perfecter: "It was fitting that God, for whom and through whom all things exist, in bringing many children to glory, should make the pioneer of their salvation perfect through sufferings" (Heb 2:10). "Although he was a Son, he learned obedience through what he suffered;

and having been made perfect, he became the source of eternal salvation for all who obey him" (Heb 5:8-9). This background contributes to the developing argument of chapter 12.

Next, the community is urged to "consider him who endured such hostility against himself from sinners, so that you might not grow weary or lose heart" (Heb 12:3). It would seem that discouragement has taken hold in the congregation as suffering has persisted or intensified, and the first three verses are intended to provide perspective. Past models of faith walked in obedience to God no matter what the circumstances. In addition, Christ himself endured suffering as a Son who "learned obedience through what he suffered" (Heb 5:8). He who endured the cross will point the way forward.

The author now presents a contrast between Christ and the community. "In your struggle against sin you have not yet resisted to the point of shedding your blood" (Heb 12:4). Unlike the pioneer, Christ, who lost his very life to the "hostility against himself from sinners," this community has not walked the path of martyrdom. They may feel discouraged or overwhelmed by their suffering, but they would do well to remember that they have not faced the ultimate test of obedience and trust—the surrender of their lifes for the sake of God.

The next verse then has the feel of a mild rebuke. The problem is that their focus on the pain of suffering has caused them to lose sight of its redemptive value. With a pertinent quote from the Septuagintal form of Proverbs 3:11-12, the author broaches a new analogy in an attempt to reframe how suffering is understood:

You have forgotten the exhortation that addresses you as children—

"My child, do not regard lightly the discipline of the Lord,
   or lose heart when you are punished by him;
 for the Lord disciplines those whom he loves,
   and chastises every child whom he accepts." (Heb 12:5-6)

Divine discipline is not to be regarded lightly, nor are they to lose heart in the midst of divine discipline. This appears to be the problem. Not only have the addressees of Hebrews failed to account for the possibility that their suffering is working to their advantage, but they are in danger of "losing heart" (which links 12:5 to 12:3) in the midst of their suffering.

Three times verses 5-6 employ the term "son" (*huios*), translated "child" by the NRSV. The congregation will only understand suffering if they hold firm to their identity as children of God. Since Jesus is the "son" (*huios*) par excellence and the pioneer of faith, we are to imitate him in this as well. For God's children, experiences of suffering are not indicative of God's disapproval or disdain. In fact, as seen in Christ, the opposite is true. Suffering is *proof* that one is God's child. Just as Jesus, the Son, "learned obedience through what he suffered," so too those who claim to be sons and daughters of God must accept that some suffering functions as discipline.

What kind of discipline is this? The Greek word translated "discipline" in this passage (*paideuō*) is directly related to the word for "child" (*paidion*). It can mean to educate, correct, give guidance, or chastise. In each case, the emphasis lies on instruction. God uses suffering in order to bring his children to maturation. God uses suffering to educate, correct, guide, and chastise his children, all the while seeking their growth and transformation. He only does this for those whom he loves and accepts, those whom he is committed to see grow into his likeness.

Hebrews 12:7a sums up the perspective that the author desires to ingrain in his audience. The Greek is stunningly simple: "Endure as discipline." The exhortation is issued as a second-person imperative. This is what you are to do: endure! The word ties together the initial exhortation to endure in 12:1 and the example of Jesus' endurance from 12:2 and 12:3. In the face of every obstacle, challenge, pain, grief and threat—endure. Endure even to the point of martyrdom, because God himself is dynamically involved in the suffering. He is using it to shape, mold, grow and refine his precious children.

Verses 7b-11 explicate the proverb and subsequent exhortation, seeking to drive home the point that suffering can be understood as discipline and discipline marks one out as a child of God. "God is treating you as children; for what child is there whom a parent does not discipline? If you do not have that discipline in which all children share, then you are illegitimate and not his children" (Heb 12:7b-8). It is not the *presence* of suffering that should prove troubling to the believer but its *absence*. If discipline is a sign of God's deep investment in our lives, then the lack of discipline shows us to be illegitimate children.

Further, if we understand the need for discipline from our human parents, shouldn't we be eager to submit to discipline from the very source of wisdom (Heb 12:9-10)? The instruction of the Lord will lead to life abundant—the life for which we were destined. Indeed, there is ultimately no comparison between our human parents and the "Father of spirits." They disciplined us "for a short time," meaning their discipline was relegated to our youth. Moreover, they disciplined "as seemed best to them." Any parent knows the struggle involved in discerning the best way to guide a child into adulthood. Decisions large and small may be made with great care, but they are ultimately no more than what seems best. In contrast, the Lord's discipline continues all the days of our lives. He always has wisdom to impart. He does not struggle to determine what is best; he already knows. He is the perfect parent, worthy of our total trust. His discipline is never frivolous or misguided; it is "for our good, so that we may share in his holiness." In other words, God's discipline seeks to grow us into his own image so that we may be worthy heirs in the royal family.

However, understanding the important role of discipline in our lives does not change the experience of it. Right perspective does not render suffering pleasant and pain-free. Suffering is suffering. There is no pleasure in it, only the secret knowledge that it is producing something marvelous. "Now, discipline always seems painful rather than pleasant at the time, but later it yields the peaceful fruit of righteousness to those who have been trained by it" (Heb 12:11). Returning to the athletic imagery of Hebrews 12:1, which portrayed the Christian life in terms of running a race, the discipline of God is depicted as a training regimen. In order to successfully run the race, you must submit to the necessary training. If you invest the energy and trust the trainer, you will make progress. For the Christian, such progress can be measured in terms of "peace" and "righteousness." Hebrews uses these two terms to describe the fruit produced by those who make progress in faith because of their submission to God's discipline. Peace and righteousness point to faith made alive in the life of the believer. Together they anticipate the ethical exhortations that will come in the following sections (compare 12:14-17; 13:1-7). Discipline makes the child more like the father—a reality that should be apparent in the believer's words and deeds. This is the "fruit" that God longs for his children to produce. In the words of Isaiah, "Then justice will dwell in the wilderness, and righteousness abide in the fruitful field. The effect of righteousness will be peace, and the result of righteousness, quiet and trust forever" (Is 32:16-17).

The author ends the Hebrews passage by reemphasizing the importance of training in verses 12 and 13. "Therefore lift your drooping hands and strengthen your weak knees, and make straight paths for your feet, so that what is lame may not be put out of joint, but rather be healed." Drooping hands and weak knees refer to Isaiah 35:3: "Strengthen the weak hands, and make firm the feeble knees." The exhortation to make straight paths echoes Proverbs 4:26: "Keep straight the path of your feet, and all your ways will be sure." Together, these exhortations refocus us on the hazards we will encounter in the race. We must endure when we feel inclined to give up, when our hands are weak and our knees are feeble. We must stick to the straight path, resisting the temptation of shortcuts and detours. If we don't, we are liable, in an already fragile state ("lameness") to become disabled ("put out of joint"). If, however, we stick to the straight path, we will find the skill and strength we need to run the good race. God himself will address our natural liabilities through his power, bringing healing to areas of wounding and weakness. Such are the benefits of his training.

REFLECTIONS

On many occasions I have asked my students to think about the most formative experiences in their lives, times when they experienced true transformation. Again and again they point to episodes of suffering. Grief, disorientation, overwhelming circumstances, persecution, physical hardship and deprivation—all serve as fertile ground for learning about God and self. In the hands of God, these experiences have the capacity to draw us near to him, to build our trust in him, to stretch us beyond our limits by bringing us to the end of our own resources. Both analogies employed in Hebrews 12 effectively drive home the important role that suffering may play in our development.

Only the hopelessly naive believe that a meaningful race can be won without training. Success in a sprint and a marathon both require commitments to a training program that will develop and grow one's natural abilities. Conditioning and strength both grow as the training program begins to pay off. However, though it offers concrete rewards, training is neither easy nor pleasant. It demands endurance in the midst of suffering.

My own efforts just to keep in shape make this clear enough. In the first time on a treadmill after a prolonged absence, the burning muscles, tight chest and cramping make me wonder if it is worthwhile. It takes a commitment of the will not to ratchet down the miles per hour, to keep the pace for a smaller amount of time. If I don't push myself, however, I know that I will remain in relatively poor shape. My conditioning will never improve, and my quality of life will diminish as I age. So I have internalized a basic truth about the treadmill: no pain, no gain. Nevertheless, it remains difficult to choose for suffering.

Hebrews 12 encourages us to see the suffering we experience as training in the only race that really matters, the race to become the persons God intended for us to be. Every obstacle has the potential to grow us. Hardship can lead us back to God, the source of our strength. God uses challenges to shape our character. Who would we be without this training? Would we ever learn compassion, humility, trust, patience or mercy? Would we ever become the people God longs for us to be?

Fortunately, God does not leave this training entirely in our own hands. We need not muster the courage to dive headlong into suffering. Frankly, I doubt if many of us would be *able* to choose for more suffering in our lives. Fortunately, the choice is not up to us. To return to the physical fitness analogy, personal trainers develop programs of exercise and map out appropriate growth goals. Most importantly, they seek the client's good even in the moments when the client is prone to forsake it. They keep the target in mind and continue to press on toward the goal, providing much-needed accountability. Two more reps, three more laps, four more crunches— on and on they urge the tired and the weary, pushing them to become all that they can be. When it comes to suffering, we have a faithful and wise trainer in God. He is deeply invested in our development and he is unwilling to sacrifice long-term growth for the sake of short-term ease. Where we see suffering, he sees opportunity, the opportunity to challenge and stretch us so that we might be better prepared to pursue the finish line with endurance, having laid aside every weight and sin that impedes us on the way to becoming who God wants us to be.

As the parent of two young children, I feel as though I understand the second analogy in ways that would have been impossible for me before. The parent who has the child's best interests at heart is often required to do things that the child considers grievous. With young children, the rationale behind such decisions is often beyond them. They are, nonetheless, in the child's best interest. While some decisions are meant to keep the child safe, most are aimed at moving the child toward greater maturity. On my daughter's first day of preschool, little boys and girls were sobbing, clinging to pant legs, desperate not to be separated from mom or dad. What if each of those parents had responded to the grief of their child by writing off school as something harmful and destructive? Clearly, some suffering is worth embracing in light of long term gains.

If God, our Father, loves us profoundly, is deeply invested in us, wants what is best for us, and knows in advance what is good for us, we should not be at all surprised that he is willing to do whatever he must for our good, even if it proves painful to us in the short term. Again, to "discipline" (*paideuō*) means to educate, correct, give guidance and chastise. Where would any of us be if our parents had refused to discipline us? Would we be better off if our heavenly Father refused to do these things on our behalf? I think not. C. S. Lewis had this to say on the subject: "He has paid us the intolerable compliment of loving us, in the deepest, most tragic, most inexorable sense. . . . It is natural for us to wish that God had designed for us a less glorious and less arduous destiny; but then we are not wishing for more love but for less."

In both of the analogies of Hebrews 12, the experience of suffering can be greatly tempered by a deeper understanding of what the suffering is intended to produce. Ideally, the person training for a race reaches the point where suffering is greeted with open arms because there is a rich history of experiencing growth on the far side of suffering, growth that could not have been attained in any other way. In the same vein, hopefully children who have reaped the benefit of wise and sober discipline eventually mature enough to see that each act of correction, instruction and chastisement has played an important role in their formation. In both cases, suffering ceases to be something to be feared and avoided. This is the perspective that Hebrews 12 seeks to instill in us.

As was the case in the earlier explorations of biblical responses to suffering, the idea of suffering as training is not without limitations. Two stand out in particular. First, we must not forget that though God can use suffering to train us, this does not mean that he causes all our suffering for the purpose of our growth and development. The analogies of God as our teacher and trainer can easily miss the mark if we draw this conclusion. Many of the situations in which God develops his people clearly exemplify God's *redemptive* work of bringing something good out of the worst circumstances. In his book *Stride Toward Freedom*, Martin Luther King describes one particularly formative episode in his development.

One night toward the end of January I settled into bed late, after a strenuous day. Coretta had already fallen asleep and just as I was about to doze off the telephone rang. An angry voice said, "Listen, nigger, we've taken all we want from you; before next week you'll be sorry you ever came to Montgomery." I hung up, but could not sleep. It seemed that all of my fears had come down on me at once. I had reached the saturation point.

I got out of bed and began to walk the floor. Finally I went to the kitchen and heated a pot of coffee. I was ready to give up. With my cup of coffee sitting untouched before me I tried to think of a way to move out of the picture without appearing a coward. In this state of exhaustion, when my courage had all but gone, I decided to take my problem to God. With my head in my hands, I bowed over the kitchen table and prayed aloud. The words I spoke to God that midnight are still vivid in my memory. "I am here taking a stand for what I believe is right. But now I am afraid. The people are looking to me for leadership, and if I stand before them without strength and courage, they too will falter. I am at the end of my powers. I have nothing left. I've come to the point where I can't face it alone."

At that moment I experienced the presence of the Divine as I had never experienced him before. It seemed as though I could hear the quiet assurance of an inner voice saying: "Stand up for righteousness, stand up for truth; and God will be at your side forever." Almost at once my fears began to go. My uncertainty disappeared. I was ready to face anything.

Three days later, while speaking at a local church, King's house was rocked by a bomb. When he arrived home, an angry crowd had gathered, ready to retaliate. The nonviolent resistance that marked the movement in Montgomery could have come crashing down in a moment. But King urged the crowd to hold to the principles of Jesus. He spoke of loving enemies and reminded them that those who live by the sword will die by the sword. Above all, the crowd was struck by King's own reaction to the bombing. The lives of his wife and child could have been snuffed out, yet he stood before them preaching the higher way of Jesus.

I do not believe that God wanted King to be threatened and his house bombed so that he could train him. But God was training King in the midst of these things. He was growing him in perseverance, dependence, courage, faith, hope and love.

The idea of suffering as training has a second limitation. The fact that God can make use of suffering should not be construed as a justification of suffering. It would be absurd to think that every sorrow and pain is worthwhile simply because it affords the opportunity for growth. For example, no matter how much God may transform the perspective of a parent who grieves the death of a child, the loss itself will never be perceived as anything less than horrific.

♦ ♦ ♦

I know of no person who so completely embraced the idea of suffering as training as Hudson Taylor, a famous missionary to China in the latter half of the 1800s. In his autobiography he writes of his preparation for life as a missionary, "It was to me a very grave matter, however, to contemplate going out to China, far away from all human aid, there to depend on the living God alone for protection, supplies, and help of every kind. I felt that one's spiritual muscles required strengthening for such an undertaking." In fact, Taylor's eagerness to grow in faith was so strong that he made a practice of not acting for himself, inviting momentary suffering in order to see God step in on his behalf.

Taylor perceived one such opportunity for growth in his regular paycheck. His employer, a good but absent-minded man, instructed Taylor to remind him when his earnings were due. Taylor resolved to place the whole matter in God's hands. He would make do with what he had until his employer remembered to pay him. He waited, and waited, and waited. He tried to stretch what little money he had left by eating only bread and water. With his money nearly gone, Taylor was beginning to feel desperate; but he was also convinced that if he were not willing to trust God to provide for him in London, he would not be equipped to trust him in China. Down to his last crown, Taylor stumbled upon a poor family in great distress. He felt God urging him to give them the last of what he had. The struggle was immense, but Taylor finally handed over that last bit of security and control. He later described the great freedom and lightness he felt in knowing that there was nothing left but to trust God. The final surrender had been the hardest, but he had truly committed himself to God's care. The next morning, Taylor's landlady handed him an envelope containing a pair of gloves and half a sovereign! The postmark was smudged and the handwriting on the envelope was indecipherable, and he never did find out who had sent it. Taylor rejoiced in God's provision and fed himself for two weeks before he was once again in dire straits. One Friday evening, Taylor was contemplating a weekend without any food, when finally his employer remembered that Taylor's pay was past due. However, he had sent all of the money to the bank! There was nothing to do until Monday. Taylor was left struggling to master his resentment and distress. Later that evening, the employer, a doctor, returned to say that one of his wealthiest patients had turned up after ten o'clock in order to pay a considerable bill. Taylor went home with the greater portion of his unpaid salary. More importantly, he went home with a renewed conviction that God would meet his needs.

I am fascinated by Hudson Taylor's training experiments. On the one hand, I am inclined to think that there are enough troubles in this life to build our faith muscles without generating fresh opportunities! On the other hand, I cannot fault Taylor's desire to grow in faith by finding opportunities to depend on God. That Taylor became a man of great faith is beyond question. His later ministry in China was utterly remarkable. Like Taylor, we all could profit from a posture of receptivity to God's training in the midst of suffering.

9

Confronting the Truth

Suffering as Testing

My first semester of college was a time of great transition. Alongside all of the normal life changes that come with moving away from home and starting college, I had a spiritual awakening. I became involved with a community of Christian believers through InterVarsity Christian Fellowship at UC Berkeley. They challenged me to place Jesus at the center of my life. Through community and Scripture and prayer, I began to learn and grow in relationship with God. Step by step my life was beginning to change.

One Sunday worship service midway through my sophomore year of college remains etched in my mind. It was an ordinary Sunday and an ordinary service, but on this occasion I had the distinct sense that God was speaking to me. He said quite simply that my personal goal of teaching history was not his goal for me. The thought came out of nowhere and a feeling of certainty blossomed in my chest. I waited with anticipation for further guidance, but there was none. I was left with a deep knowing that God had other plans for me, and he was asking me to be open to them.

God had put me in an awkward spot. Until then, my path had seemed clear enough. I have always loved history. The task of choosing a major in college was not difficult for me, and my interest translated into success in the classroom. But now God was redirecting me, prompting me to set aside the future I imagined for myself. It would have been a great deal easier if God had given me some tangible sense of what he had in mind. Instead, I was left with a choice between pursuing my own concrete plan and trusting in God. It felt like a test. Would I give up control, the assurance that comes from knowing where I am going and exactly what I need to do to get there? Would I wait on God to direct me in his time? Would I trust the one who had been revealing himself to me in dynamic ways over the past year and a half? I chose to trust.

Without an obvious alternative, I continued with my history major the next two years, all the while knowing that I would not pursue a vocation teaching history. Regularly I had to submit my doubts and anxieties to God. Waiting on God was not easy, especially as graduation drew near and I had no greater sense of what God desired. However, my posture of expectant waiting was a constant reminder of my willingness to trust God. In this case, I am certain that my trust was all he wanted.

Ultimately, the process of discovering the path God would set me on proved rather undramatic compared to the test God put before me that Sunday in my sophomore year. If his "no" came like a lightning bolt, his "yes" entered my life slowly and surely like a cloud moving in from the horizon. In the end, I am grateful for the test God put before me. In enabled me to see that I could indeed surrender my life to him.

EXODUS 17:1-7

[1] From the wilderness of Sin the whole congregation of the Israelites journeyed by stages, as the LORD commanded. They camped at Rephidim, but there was no water for the people to drink. [2] The people quarreled with Moses, and said, "Give us water to drink." Moses said to them, "Why do you quarrel with me? Why do you test the LORD?" [3] But the people thirsted there for water; and the people complained against Moses and said, "Why did you bring us out of Egypt, to kill us and our children and livestock with thirst?" [4] So Moses cried out to the LORD, "What shall I do with this people? They are almost ready to stone me." [5] The LORD said to Moses, "Go on ahead of the people, and take some of the elders of Israel with you; take in your hand the staff with which you struck the Nile, and go. [6] I will be standing there in front of you on the rock at Horeb. Strike the rock, and water will come out of it, so that the people may drink." Moses did so, in the sight of the elders of Israel. [7] He called the place Massah and Meribah, because the Israelites quarreled and tested the LORD, saying, "Is the LORD among us or not?"

How does God discern depth of commitment, genuineness of faith, consistency of character, reality of hope? These things are not just cultivated but also proven in the refining fire of suffering. Satan is not the only one to test the people of God with suffering. God also initiates such tests. Granted, the aim is different. Satan tests with suffering in order to cripple faith, undermining the life-giving support that derives from relationship with God. By contrast, tests that come from God are a vital part of self-discovery. They have the potential to lay bare truths about ourselves (both good and bad) that we failed to recognize before we were faced with adversity. The testing of God makes it plain how far we have come and how far we need to go.

For example, when a child is learning how to swim, time is initially spent adjusting to the water. It is normal for a child who has never been in a pool to cling to the parent. Gradually the child feels freer to explore movement in the water while supported by the parent. Eventually, however, the time comes for the parent to let go. This "test" will reveal whether the child has indeed learned enough to swim. The test is real, and the challenge concrete. The child will either swim or sink. There is no other way to know whether real progress toward the goal has been made. In this example, however, it is important to note that the child is not left to drown. God, like the parent, intervenes on behalf of his child. Failure to reach the intended goal opens up the possibility of further instruction. This is the kind of testing we see unfold in Exodus 17:1-7.

This is the final passage in a sequence that begins in 15:22. By this point, Israel has experienced the great liberation of the exodus. They have seen God rain down destruction on mighty Egypt, as plague after plague brought the empire to its knees. They passed through the sea on dry land and watched the same waters Moses had parted crash down upon the pursuing chariots and soldiers of Egypt. The people have begun a new phase in their journey. With Egypt behind them and the land of promise ahead, the people find themselves in the ambiguity of the wilderness. As Exodus 15:22–17:7 makes plain, the wilderness is a place of testing. What has Israel learned of her God? Has Israel learned to "swim"?

In Exodus 15:22 the people come to Marah, where they find the water undrinkable. Immediately fear gets the best of them. They are confronted with a real need—a test. The Israelites, who have seen God meet their needs in dramatic fashion so far, are encouraged to trust that he will do so once again. However, rather than seize the opportunity to see how God will move on their behalf, they lift their voices to Moses in complaint. "And the people complained against Moses, saying, 'What shall we drink?'" (Ex 15:24). God, the patient parent, does not withhold the water that the people need. He instructs Moses to throw a piece of wood in the water, which miraculously changes it from bitter to sweet.

This first episode is followed by commentary that makes explicit what the Lord intends to accomplish through this wilderness experience.

> There the LORD made for them a statute and an ordinance and there he *put them to the test.* He said, "If you will listen carefully to the voice of the LORD your God, and do what is right in his sight, and give heed to his commandments and keep all his statutes, I will not bring upon you any of the diseases that I brought upon the Egyptians; for I am the LORD who heals you." (Ex 15:25-26, emphasis added)

The complete statutes and ordinances will be revealed to Moses on Mount Sinai, but already Israel is told what is expected of her in summary fashion: to listen carefully to the voice of the Lord and to do what is right in his sight. Exodus 15:22–17:7 includes a series of tests intended to discern whether Israel has come to trust the Lord their God in this fashion.

The next test involves a need for food. Just one month after leaving Egypt, "The whole congregation of the Israelites complained against Moses and Aaron in the wilderness. The Israelites said to them, 'If only we had died by the hand of the LORD in the land of Egypt, when we sat by the fleshpots and ate our fill of bread; for you have brought us out into this wilderness to kill this whole assembly with hunger" (Ex 16:2-3). The content of their complaint is shocking. In a short time they have already romanticized their time of slavery in Egypt and forgotten the Lord's provision of drinkable water in the wilderness. To add insult to injury, they suggest that the Egyptians who were killed by the Lord's dramatic liberating activity were ultimately better off than themselves—better a quick death than a long, painful one.

God responds to this complaint with provision. He sends manna and quail from heaven, and once again gives Israel the opportunity to listen to his voice and do what is right in his eyes. Israel must gather enough manna for only one day, saving none for the next day. On the day before the Sabbath, however, a double portion is to be gathered, and no manna will come on the Sabbath. "In that way I will test them, whether they will follow my instruction or not" (Ex 16:4). This time the test does not directly involve suffering. Rather, it includes the *possibility* of suffering if God does not remain true to his word to deliver *daily* manna. These baby steps are tests designed to cultivate faith. In spite of these explicit instructions, Israel fails to obey God's command on both counts. Unwilling or unable to trust that God would deliver manna the following day, some within Israel attempt to keep a portion of their provision for the next morning only to find that it had bred worms and become foul. On the seventh day, after gathering double the portion of manna the day before, some within Israel still go out to gather manna on the Sabbath but find none. This time the failure elicits a rebuke from God: "How long will you refuse to keep my commandments and instructions?" (Ex 16:28).

Exodus 17:1-7 is, then, the final wilderness test before Sinai. The Israelites continue on their long wilderness trek and camp at Rephidim, where they are confronted with a familiar problem. "There was no water for the people to drink" (Ex 17:1). How will they respond to this latest deprivation? Have they learned from his gift of sweet water at Marah? Have they learned from his provision of manna and quail? Israel faces a test once more, an opportunity to demonstrate growth, to lay hold of a new level of trust in their God.

Israel's response comes almost like a reflex in the very next line. "The people quarreled with Moses, and said, 'Give us water to drink'" (Ex 17:2). They fail to recognize even the opportunity to trust the

Lord. Instead, they state their demands. The Hebrew *riv* ("quarrel") is often used of Hebrew judicial proceedings. The Israelites, finding no water, hold Moses, God's representative, responsible. He must produce water or pay the consequences (compare Ex 17:4, where Moses tells God that "they are almost ready to stone me").

Moses is caught between a God intent on testing his people's faith and an apparently faithless people. "Why do you quarrel with me? Why do you test the Lord?" he asks (Ex 17:2). Whether they realize it or not, their dispute against Moses is really a dispute against God (compare Ex 16:8). Moses is nothing more than a servant. He goes where the Lord tells him to go. He does what the Lord tells him to do. Hence, when the Israelites make demands of Moses they are really making demands of God. They are testing their God.

Rather than responding to God's prompting to grow in faith, Israel seeks to set the terms of relationship with him. Suffering is interpreted as God's absence or negligence. The great irony is that God's testing of Israel, intended to bring her into deeper levels of relationship and maturity, has given way to Israel's testing of God, an entirely inappropriate subversion of the parent-child relationship. Like a child throwing a tantrum, defiant Israel tells God in no uncertain terms what it means to be a good father. Unable to see past her own need, Israel cannot trust that there might be a greater good in her suffering.

Moses' questions have fallen on deaf ears as the complaint continues: "Why did you bring us out of Egypt, to kill us and our children and livestock with thirst?" (Ex 17:5). The Israelites have begun questioning the very character of God and his servant Moses. It is stunning that God's previous activity on their behalf has engendered so little goodwill. He heard their cry for rescue from slavery in Egypt and he delivered them. He heard their cry for water at Marah and he gave them water to drink. He heard their cry for bread and meat and he gave them manna and quail. How can they accuse Moses of bringing them into the desert in order to kill them? The utter self-absorption of the Israelites is further highlighted in the original Hebrew through the use of the first-person singular. Instead of the "*us* and *our* children and livestock" of the NRSV, the Hebrew literally reads, "Why did you bring us out of Egypt, to kill *me*, and *my* children and *my* livestock with thirst?" The image is of a nation speaking with a single voice of complaint, and Moses is at his wits' end. The people have turned against him once again, demanding from him what he does not have the power to deliver. This time, he concludes, "They are almost ready to stone me" (Ex 17:4).

In his response, God does not address their lack of faith. He does not address their failure to have learned from past events. He does not even address their slanderous accusations. Instead, he moves to meet their need. Moses is to go to the "rock at Horeb" accompanied by some of the elders of Israel. There he will strike the rock and water will issue forth. The instructions are laden with meaning. First, the plan involves some of the elders of Israel. Moses is instructed to bring them along in Exodus 17:5, and in the next verse they are called to be witnesses of the event: "Moses did so in the sight of the elders of Israel" (Ex 17:6). The Lord is continuing to teach his people that he will provide for them. In doing so, he seeks to inculcate trust where it is lacking.

Second, Moses is told to take in his hand "the staff with which you struck the Nile" (Ex 17:5). Just as Israel saw Moses use his staff to turn the Nile into blood, rendering it unfit for drinking, so they will now see him miraculously bring forth water from a rock using the same staff. The message is clear. God has been at work in Israel's past to harm their enemies. Now he works in the present to meet their needs.

Third, God tells Moses, "I will be standing there in front of you on the rock at Horeb" (Ex 17:6). We see that the wilderness tests are drawing to a close. God will provide water when they reach the rock at Horeb, also known as Mount Sinai. It would seem that Rephidim is quite near to Horeb. Israel is at the very threshold of their new life with God. At Horeb the law will be given to Moses, and the people will enter into covenant with the Lord. At Horeb, the trust that God has been seeking to nourish and grow in Egypt and in the wilderness will be expected of his covenant people. The wilderness tests were preparation for this new identity.

For Moses, Horeb is a reminder of God's past, present and future faithfulness. It was at Horeb that God appeared to Moses in a burning bush, calling him to perform a seemingly impossible mission. "I will be with you" God told him, "and this shall be the sign for you that it is I who sent you: when you have brought the people out of Egypt, you shall worship God on this mountain" (Ex 3:12). At Horeb, Moses had faced his own tests of faith. He raised a string of objections when initially encountered by God. He requested the name of God in order to convince the Hebrews that the God of their ancestors had spoken to him. He continued to doubt that the Hebrews would listen, so God gave him signs to perform. He doubted his adequacy for the task, claiming to be slow of speech and slow of tongue. The Lord assured Moses that the right words would be given to him. Finally, he said simply, "O my Lord, please send someone else" (Ex 4:13). God, though perturbed, agreed that Aaron would accompany Moses. As the narrative of Exodus proceeds, though, the reticence and fear with which he met God's initial demands melt away. Moses returns to Horeb as a faithful servant, one who can testify to the miraculous redemptive work of God on behalf of his people and in his own life. Moses sees clearly that his own life of faith has brought him safely back to Horeb, just as God told him.

However, it is not just God's past and present faithfulness that are in view in this passage. The next step for Moses and his people is clearly alluded to as well. God tells Moses that they will meet at the rock: "I will be standing there in front of you" (Ex 17:6). This prefigures the encounter that they will have on Mount Sinai, when Moses will meet with God for forty days and receive the law on behalf of the people.

When Moses arrives at the rock and strikes it with his staff, water pours forth in the presence of the elders of Israel. Moses then re-names Rephidim "Massah and Meribah"—which mean "test" and "quarrel," respectively—"because the Israelites quarreled and tested the LORD, saying, 'Is the LORD among us or not?'" (Ex 17:7). This final question is the perfect summary of the wilderness tests described in Exodus 15:22–17:7. Israel has interpreted every privation, every suffering and every pain in terms of forsakenness. Experiences of hunger and thirst are seen as sure signs that the Lord has abandoned his people—or worse yet, that he intends evil for them. For his part, the Lord seeks to test and grow their fledgling faith. Moments of suffering are opportunities to trust that God is still present, to trust that God is good, to trust that God has plans and purposes, to trust that God will provide what is needed when it is needed. This trust is only revealed in the crucible of suffering.

The episode at Massah and Meribah remains a strong reminder of the faith God sought from the wilderness generation and the subsequent testing and quarreling he received. Several Old Testament passages reflect on the events of Exodus 17:1-7, including Deuteronomy 6:16 and Psalms 78, 81, and 95. In addition, Numbers 20 relays a very similar story that involves Moses bringing forth water from a rock at Meribah. It was an important episode in Israel's history.

Particularly noteworthy are Psalm 78 and Psalm 81. Psalm 78, in recalling the manner in which the wilderness generation put God to the test (though in a different sequence), makes it clear that God was seeking a response of faith and trust.

> They tested God in their heart
>   by demanding the food they craved.
> They spoke against God, saying,
>   "Can God spread a table in the wilderness?
> Even though he struck the rock so that water gushed out
>   and torrents overflowed,
> can he also give bread,
>   or provide meat for his people?"
>
> Therefore, when the LORD heard, he was full of rage;
>   a fire was kindled against Jacob,
>   his anger mounted against Israel,
> because they had no *faith* in God,
>   and did not *trust* his saving power.
>   (Ps 78:18-22, emphasis added)

Psalm 81 rightly adduces that the testing at Massah and Meribah was first and foremost the testing of Israel by God:

> In distress you called, and I rescued you;
>   I answered you in the secret place of thunder;
>   *I tested you* at the waters of Meribah.
>   (Ps 81:7, emphasis added)

The New Testament also includes a significant reference to Exodus 17 in 1 Corinthians 10. Paul warns the Corinthian congregation that they are not exempt from judgment. He reminds them of the special privileges of the wilderness generation. They too shared in events that functioned as a "baptism" in their journey of faith: "All were baptized into Moses in the cloud and the sea" (1 Cor 10:2). They too shared in "spiritual food" and "spiritual drink" akin to the Lord's Supper: "For they drank from the spiritual rock that followed them, and the rock was Christ" (1 Cor 10:4). By identifying the rock with Christ, Paul encourages the Corinthians to understand that their experience is not unique. God's miraculous activity in the past can be understood in light of Christ's provision as well. If that is the case, then Christians should take careful note of the fate of the wilderness generation. "Nevertheless, God was not pleased with most of them, and they were struck down in the wilderness" (1 Cor 10:5). Not surprisingly, this section concludes with some reflections on testing. "No testing has overtaken you that is not common to everyone. God is faithful, and he will not let you be tested beyond your strength, but with the testing he will also provide a way out so that you may be able to endure it" (1 Cor 10:13). Testing remains a common instrument in the life of faith. Suffering reveals how far we have come in our ability to trust God—and how far we still have to go.

Reflections

Nearly my entire life has been lived in relationship to school. After twenty-four years as a student, I simply moved in front of the class when I became a professor. Though my days as a test-taker are over, I am now responsible for scheduling, writing and grading tests. Being on this side of the process has afforded me a different perspective. Though the tests I administer are trivial compared to the tests we face in our lives of faith, there are some interesting points of connection.

For starters, preparation makes all the difference between success and failure. If you know a test is coming and prepare for it, you stand a good chance of performing admirably. Unfortunately, we do not have the luxury of circling a date on our calendars for the next life test God may send our way, but preparation is still crucial. The wilderness generation failed to prepare themselves, and they were bewildered every time they encountered a new test. They failed to learn and grow, resolving to trust the God who had proven himself trustworthy. Instead, every new test produced shock, dismay and ultimately despair.

Tests also play an important role in keeping students accountable. Knowing that a test is coming encourages them to continue investing in the course even in those moments when the "spirit is willing but the flesh is weak." With all of the demands placed on their lives, the accountability gained through testing ensures that they are continuing to learn the things that will serve them well in the future. In fact, I have found that it is important to have a rhythm to tests that I administer in my classes. Students can easily grow complacent if they are not being spurred on. In a sense, each test focuses their eyes on the horizon, calling them to take the next step in the learning process. Perhaps God tests us in a similar way, shaking us out of complacency with a test of our faith, encouraging us to grow, learn and take stock of ourselves in the process. I wonder if any of us would make substantial progress in the life of faith without such regular challenges. No matter what the outcome, they do us a service. Sometimes a test will reveal to us how much we have matured in Christ, giving us an opportunity to celebrate and feel encouraged about the work God is doing in our lives. Other times a test will show us how far we still have to go in our journey with God, exposing as a farce the pretenses we were clinging to. In this way tests help us to stay grounded in reality and to develop a realistic assessment of ourselves.

Before I became a professor, I heard many stories about the tedium of grading. Tests were described as a necessary evil, a constant drain on the professor's time. But I discovered that I genuinely enjoy grading tests. Certainly the repetitive nature of the task is often less than stimulating, but I continue to find myself eager to see how the next student will perform. Each test offers me a glimpse into what a student learned, and I know that this new knowledge contains the seed of something much greater: genuine transformation. I imagine that God watches over every new test that we face with similar anticipation. He is eager to see whether we have learned and grown. After all, he is deeply invested in both the process and the outcome.

God-given tests have always played a key role in the life of faith. For example, Abraham and Sarah's commitment was tested as they waited long years for God to grant them their promised son. They were tested again when God asked Abraham to bind his son Isaac and offer him as a sacrifice. They proved themselves worthy of the covenant God made with them, becoming examples of faith to all who follow in their footsteps. The tests God puts in our lives, while likely less intense, will likewise reveal truth about our discipleship.

A final warning is appropriate as we wrap up our exploration of divine testing. As valuable as tests might be, it would be misguided to assume that every challenge and experience of suffering is a test from God. As always when it comes to suffering, we must be open to hearing the entire harmony that is the scriptural witness.

10

Jars of Clay

*Suffering and the
Power of Weakness*

✝

It would have been fun to listen in on Moses' "job interview" at the burning bush:

> You've got the wrong guy, God. I can't think of a worse candidate for the job. I haven't been to Egypt in years. I'm a wanted man there. You do know I fled in order to save my life, right? You need someone full of courage to pull off that kind of job! Besides, I'm settled now. I've established a new life in Midian. I finally know who I am and where I belong. I have a family of my own. Even if I did go, why would they follow my lead? I may be a Hebrew, but I'm still an outsider. It would be far better to select someone who is already a respected voice in the community. Do you even know about my speech problem, God? Do you think Pharaoh is going to be swayed when I stand before him stammering? For your sake and mine, God, please send someone else!

There were so many reasons for God to choose someone else, but God chose Moses. God knew what Moses could become. Certainly

Moses had many strengths waiting to be discovered, but God embraced Moses' weaknesses as well. Moses seemed an unlikely candidate to lead the people of God to freedom because he was! The deficiencies he laid before God were real. They were a source of difficulty and sorrow for Moses, but God saw them as opportunities to reveal his power and glory.

2 CORINTHIANS 4:7-12

> [7] But we have this treasure in clay jars, so that it may be made clear that this extraordinary power belongs to God and does not come from us. [8] We are afflicted in every way, but not crushed; perplexed, but not driven to despair; [9] persecuted, but not forsaken; struck down, but not destroyed; [10] always carrying in the body the death of Jesus, so that the life of Jesus may also be made visible in our bodies. [11] For while we live, we are always being given up to death for Jesus' sake, so that the life of Jesus may be made visible in our mortal flesh. [12] So death is at work in us, but life in you.

Second Corinthians dwells deeply on the mystery of suffering for two reasons. First, Paul had recently escaped from an immensely perilous situation. His circumstances were so grim that he anticipated his own death. "We do not want you to be unaware, brothers and sisters, of the affliction we experienced in Asia; for we were so utterly, unbearably crushed that we despaired of life itself" (2 Cor 1:8). Paul learned much from this experience, and it gave shape to a great deal of what he would share in this letter. Second, suffering is for Paul the principal proof of his apostolic authority. Paul's opponents in Corinth, whom he sarcastically terms "super-apostles," revel in their own powers and abilities. In contrast, Paul asserts that weakness manifested in suffering is the true mark of the disciple.

Our passage, 2 Corinthians 4:7-12, seeks to uncover the purpose of our weakness and how it gives shape to the life of faith.

In 2 Corinthians 3:7–4:6, Paul spoke at length about "the gospel of the glory of Christ, who is the image of God" (2 Cor 4:4), including the way this glory is renewing and transforming the believer: "All of us, with unveiled faces, seeing the glory of the Lord as though reflected in a mirror, are being transformed into the same image from one degree of glory to another" (2 Cor 3:18).

But the life of the believer is anything but "glory," and Paul addresses this sobering reality in our passage. "But we have this treasure in clay jars." The treasure that we have is none other than the gospel of glory, described in the previous line as "the knowledge of the glory of God in the face of Jesus Christ" (2 Cor 4:6). It has been entrusted to us so that we might carry this greatest of treasures into the world, making the glory known to all. This treasure is in clay jars, which in antiquity were both fragile and inexpensive. They were used for common household tasks. Clay jars were not meant to be admired or even noticed. They were the essence of utility, their sole value lying in their functionality. We are the clay jars—fragile, inconspicuous, lacking intrinsic honor. Our bodies are feeble, our abilities lacking, our power limited. We are weak, and in our weakness we are susceptible to every form of suffering.

However, in God's divine purposes this very weakness becomes an asset. God places his treasure in clay jars "*so that* it may be made clear that this extraordinary power belongs to God and does not come from us." Clay jars are the perfect vessel for God's gospel because they are different from the glorious gospel that they hold. When, in their frailty, they manifest something of the glory and power of God, it is evident to all that this glory and power have come from the treasure that they bear. The humility of the messenger highlights the magnificence of the message.

For this reason, those who have received Christ continue to walk in weakness, exposed to every kind of suffering, set apart only by virtue of the wonder that they bear. Paul describes the suffering of the disciple in a series of four antitheses: "We are afflicted in every way, but not crushed; perplexed, but not driven to despair; persecuted, but not forsaken; struck down, but not destroyed" (2 Cor 4:8-9). The first term in each corresponds to the suffering that we can expect as followers of Christ. While this suffering is common to all of humanity, it is apparently normative for the life of the Christian. It is, oddly enough, a sign of God's presence. The second term in each antithesis reveals the power of God working to preserve the believer. As weakness and suffering abound, God's saving activity abounds all the more.

It is difficult to capture the sense of the four antitheses in English. The first consists of two terms (*thlibomenoi* and *stenochōroumenoi*) associated with being crushed or pressed. They differ only in degree. Though the pressure may be intense, the vessel remains intact.

The second involves a play on words in the Greek. The believer is literally "at a loss" (*aporoumenoi*), but is not "completely at a loss" (*exaporoumenoi*). This antithesis is fascinating in light of Paul's earlier statement that, while under persecution in the Roman province of Asia, he had "despaired (*exaporēthēnai*, from the same root) of life itself" (2 Cor 1:8). We see here a hint that Paul's theology of suffering as expressed in 2 Corinthians was born out of this difficult situation. Though his suffering seemed to point to certain death, God had rescued him from peril. He had not, in fact, been completely at a loss. All things are possible with God, and he often acts when things seem the most bleak.

The third antithesis warns that the believer should expect persecution (*diōkomenoi*). No matter how severe the persecution, believers can take comfort in the fact that they will never be forsaken (*egkataleipomenoi*) by God. This latter term resonates with earlier promises of God not to forsake his people. As God spoke to Jacob at Bethel, "Know that I am with you and will keep you wherever you go, and I will bring you back to this land; for I will not leave (*egkatalipō*) you until I have done what I promised you" (Gen 28:15 Septuagint; compare Deut 31:6, 8; Ps 37:25, 28).

The final pairing asserts that though believers may be "struck down" (*kataballomenoi*), they will not be "destroyed" (*apollymenoi*). What believers are saved from here is not death but eschatological destruction. No matter how terrible the blow, believers' lives rest secure in God's hands. Even death cannot separate them from Jesus.

These four antitheses are summed up in a final line: "Always carrying in the body the death of Jesus, so that the life of Jesus may also be made visible in our bodies" (2 Cor 4:10). The weakness of the believer that reveals the power of God is a weakness that even Jesus knew. He also suffered. He also was crushed, confounded, persecuted and struck down. The Greek word used here for death (*nekrōsis*; which occurs only twice in the New Testament) is not the normal word for death (*thanatos*). This word emphasizes the *process* of dying and points to Jesus' decisions, large and small, to embrace suffering. This was the path he chose, and it led straight to the cross. We who bear his name follow in his way. To be filled with the remarkable treasure of the gospel is to carry the death of Jesus— to identify with it, submit to it and make it our own. We do so because in this state of weakness the true power of God is made known. Just as the crucifixion led to resurrection, so too will those who experience the dying of Jesus know the life of Jesus. Hence the life of the believer recapitulates the heart of the gospel message. Crucifixion and resurrection are daily realities for the believer. As we die with Christ, we are raised with Christ. As we submit to suffering in his name, we experience God's miraculous life-giving power. As Paul will assert at a later point in 2 Corinthians, "So I will boast all the more gladly of my weakness, so that the power of Christ may dwell in me. Therefore I am content with weaknesses, insults, hardships, persecutions, and calamities for the sake of Christ; for whenever I am weak, then I am strong" (2 Cor 12:9-10).

The next verse rephrases the conclusion of verse 10, driving home the point. "For while we live, we are always being given up to death for Jesus' sake, so that the life of Jesus may be made visible in our mortal flesh" (2 Cor 4:11). Two things are interesting about this restatement. First, Paul implies that there is a mysterious spiritual axiom at work. The life-giving power of God is released into the life of the believer when death is present, just as it was for Jesus. Hence we are "given up" (*paradidometha*) to death by God *so that* we might know his life. Like it or not, weakness and the suffering it brings are necessary preconditions for experiencing resurrection life. Jesus' description of the life of discipleship rings true: "If any want to become my followers, let them deny themselves and take up their cross and follow me" (Mk 8:34). Second, the life of Jesus is made visible (*phanerōthē*) in our mortal flesh. Apparently, the resurrection life that proceeds from God in our moment of need is not for us alone. It is made known to others as well, a powerful witness to all who have eyes to see. Because it is received in weakness, it is clear to everyone that "this extraordinary power belongs to God and does not come from us." Such is the advantage of clay jars.

The final line reinforces the notion that the believer's experience of Jesus' death and life involve much more than the individual. "So death is at work in us, but life in *you*" (2 Cor 4:12). The resurrection power of Jesus far outpaces the experience of death. It means not only deliverance for the believer but the power of God loosed upon the world.

REFLECTIONS

Let's not kid ourselves. We do not value weakness. We try to hide it, overcome it, deny it. It makes us uncomfortable, vulnerable and self-conscious. Everything around us reinforces the idea that weakness is bad. As a culture, we proclaim loudly and boldly that our heroes are the strong, the beautiful, the intelligent and the talented. When we apply for a job we construct a flawless presentation of ourselves called a résumé, and we rehearse answers to questions in a manner calculated to highlight our every sterling attribute. We strive for the upper hand and attempt to climb the social ladder, the professional ladder and any other ladder we can lay our hands on. We do it all because we want to respect ourselves and be admired by others.

In the midst of this, Paul speaks his discordant words of weakness and death. He tells us that God hopes for us what we have so earnestly been trying to avoid. He chastens our attempts to elevate our own reputation, telling us frankly that they only serve to diminish God's. Our pledge must be none other than that of John the Baptist, who proclaimed, "He must increase, but I must decrease" (Jn 3:30). In our weakness we experience the living God, and in our weakness he uses us to change the world. For when our weakness is evident, the "game" comes to an end. We stop pretending to be something that we are not—that we are anything at all outside of God. When we embrace our weaknesses we crack open the door to reality, making it possible for God's power to shine through.

Since weakness is a defining feature of life with God, Christians should *expect* that life will bring a measure of suffering. Suffering reminds us that we are weak and in need of God, though the world presses us to assert ourselves. Suffering opens up new possibilities for God to work in us and through us. Suffering reminds us that when death abounds, resurrection is also present.

In 1967, seventeen-year-old Joni Eareckson dove into a murky lake that would change her life. Her head violently struck the bottom of the lake, rendering her paralyzed from the shoulders down. The next two years of her life she was in a deep depression. Every dream had been stripped away. She was painfully aware that she lacked control over her body, her life, her future. She did not even have the power to kill herself, though she longed to do so. Joni was confronted with the full measure of her weakness. I am not suggesting that God brought about Joni's terrible accident, but God did bring good out of Joni's tragedy. He used her weakness to minister to her and to others. As Joni came to grips with the new circumstances of her life, God moved into the center. He was able to sustain her, give her direction and perspective and show her where her real value lay, all because of her accident. Joni's physical limitations opened up a new life with God. As Joni put it, "Before my accident, I didn't 'need' Christ. Now I needed him desperately." Moreover, the accident that put an end to all of her seventeen-year-old dreams was the seedbed of a whole new set of dreams. Joni has become a champion for the disabled, a potent minister of the gospel, a widely read author and a wonderful artist. Truly, we carry a great treasure in these clay jars.

11

Pass It On

Suffering and the Comfort of God

✝

Tim was forty-five years old when he began experiencing an odd weakening in his right leg. It lasted for several weeks but he brushed it off, assuming he had simply strained something. It wasn't until the church softball game that he knew he needed to see a doctor. He hit the ball and was rounding first base when he temporarily lost vision. Filled with panic but not wanting to cause a scene, Tim called for a replacement and stumbled off the field. A feeling of dread welled up inside him as his wife took him to the emergency room. After tests, more tests, and even more tests, Tim finally had a diagnosis: multiple sclerosis.

Pain became Tim's new companion, but the physical challenges brought on by the disease were only part of the story. Tim's future, which had felt so secure, was up in the air. Would he be able to continue in his job? How would his role as a husband and a father change? How quickly would the disease progress? Tim was aware that he was becoming a different person: Tim with MS. What would life be like for this new Tim?

Along with all the other questions and problems, Tim was filled with a deep sense of alienation. For the first time in his life, he felt truly alone. He didn't know how his community would relate to this new person whose life had veered dramatically off course. Would his loved ones recognize him garbed in the grief that was now his daily companion? Was there still a place for hope, for joy?

2 CORINTHIANS 1:3-7

> [3] Blessed be the God and Father of our Lord Jesus Christ, the Father of mercies and the God of all consolation, [4] who consoles us in all our affliction, so that we may be able to console those who are in any affliction with the consolation with which we ourselves are consoled by God. [5] For just as the sufferings of Christ are abundant for us, so also our consolation is abundant through Christ. [6] If we are being afflicted, it is for your consolation and salvation; if we are being consoled, it is for your consolation, which you experience when you patiently endure the same sufferings that we are also suffering. [7] Our hope for you is unshaken; for we know that as you share in our sufferings, so also you share in our consolation.

We have seen that Paul's second letter to the Corinthians contains a great deal of reflection on the nature of suffering as a disciple of Christ. In the last chapter we explored his meditations on the relationship between weakness and suffering. Another avenue for exploration is the one found in this passage: the comfort God brings in tribulation. God is not passive as his children face hardships. It is in his nature to meet us in our suffering, to pour out on us the consolation we so desperately need. In this overflowing comfort, Paul recognizes another hidden benefit of suffering. For the one whose sorrows multiply, the consolation of God multiplies. But it doesn't end there. Once received, the consolation of God may be poured out on others. The one who has received comfort becomes an agent of comfort to others, applying the divine salve of God's restoring touch to all those who suffer.

Fresh from his experience of severe hardship in Asia (2 Cor 1:8-9), Paul is acutely aware of the comfort of God in his own life, and he is keen to share this comfort with the Corinthians so that they might profit from his affliction. Paul is so eager to share with the Corinthians that he forgoes his typical thanksgiving for the congregation he is addressing. Instead, he launches into a reflective benediction extolling the wonderful comfort of God: "Blessed be the God and Father of our Lord Jesus Christ, the Father of mercies and the God of all consolation" (2 Cor 1:3). Paul intends to highlight two aspects of God's character. The same God who sent his Son, the Lord Jesus Christ, to show us mercy and console us in our affliction is in his very *nature* the father of mercies and the God of all consolation. We know what to expect from God. He is true to his character.

Mercy and consolation as attributes of God both have a rich background in the Old Testament. Mercy is one of the attributes listed in God's elaboration of the divine name to Moses in Exodus, "The LORD, the LORD, a God merciful and gracious" (Ex 34:6). The psalmists regularly make appeals to God based on his mercy. However, it is "consolation"(*paraklēsis*), that 2 Corinthians 1:3-7 explores in great detail. Various forms of *paraklēsis* appear ten times in this passage. *Paraklēsis* can be translated a variety of ways depending on context, but the combination of three English words offers the best depiction of its meaning in our passage: *comfort, consolation* and *encouragement*. Many of the psalms draw on the understanding that consolation and encouragement are found in God. Among them are the famous words of Psalm 23, "Even though I walk through the darkest valley, I fear no evil; for you are with me; your rod and your staff—they comfort me" (Ps 23:4).

The *paraklēsis* of God renews and refreshes our spirits, giving us hope in the midst of despair, courage in the midst of fear, strength in the midst of weakness, faith in the midst of doubt. His *paraklēsis* enables us to see the unfolding trials of our lives from his perspective so that we might persevere when facing hardships. His *paraklēsis* enables us to see ourselves from his perspective so that we might live up to our calling in Christ.

But there is more. The Father of all mercies and the God of all consolation is also at work in the world on our behalf. There is good reason to believe that when Paul speaks of God's *paraklēsis*, he also has in mind God's saving power, his capacity to deliver his children from crisis. To begin with, there is precedent in both the Old and New Testaments for such usage. Isaiah 40–66 speaks of God's restoration of his people Israel. God has come to act on their behalf, to do a new thing in the life of his suffering people. The opening lines of this grand promise declare that the time for comfort has come: "Comfort, O comfort my people, says your God" (Is 40:1). Many centuries later, a Jew named Simeon longed for God to intervene again. "Now there was a man in Jerusalem whose name was Simeon; this man was righteous and devout, looking forward to the consolation of Israel, and the Holy Spirit rested on him" (Lk 2:25).

Paul too had experienced God's comfort in all of its wondrous facets, and he blesses God for this very reason. God had comforted and encouraged him in the darkest valleys. A catalogue of Paul's more grievous sufferings reads like a manifesto on suffering.

> Five times I have received from the Jews the forty lashes minus one. Three times I was beaten with rods. Once I received a stoning. Three times I was shipwrecked; for a night and a day I was adrift at sea; on frequent journeys, in danger from rivers, danger from bandits, danger from my own people, danger from Gentiles, danger in the city, danger in the wilderness, danger at sea, danger from false brothers and sisters; in toil and hardship, through many a sleepless night, hungry

and thirsty, often without food, cold and naked. And, besides
other things, I am under daily pressure because of my anxiety
for all the churches. Who is weak, and I am not weak? Who
is made to stumble, and I am not indignant? (2 Cor 11:24-29)

Yet Paul stands tall, having weathered each storm with God's aid.
God's mercy and consolation are not mere abstractions for Paul.
They have supported him time and time again, breathing new hope
and life into him in the moments of greatest despair. As hard as it
is to imagine, it would seem that his most recent experience in the
Roman province of Asia was the direst of his career. "We were so
utterly, unbearably crushed that we despaired of life itself. Indeed,
we felt that we had received the sentence of death" (2 Cor 1:8-9). Yet
even in Asia the comfort of God found Paul. It came in the form of
deliverance from harm, which Paul equates with the resurrection
power of God. So Paul asserts, "He who rescued us from so deadly
a peril will continue to rescue us; on him we have set our hope that
he will rescue us again" (2 Cor 1:10).

Paul's principal interest in our passage is to convince the Corinthian congregation that this consolation he has received is of great
benefit to them. He continues by describing the Father of mercies
and the God of all consolation as the one "who consoles us in all
our affliction, so that we may be able to console those who are in
any affliction with the consolation with which we ourselves are consoled by God" (2 Cor 1:4). One purpose of God's consolation is to
prepare the recipient to administer that consolation to others who
are in need of it.

The consolation remains God's. It comes from him and relies solely
on his power. Only he can enliven hearts, encourage downcast spirits
and deliver his children from crisis. But the glorious mystery is that
he extends these things through others who have received his consolation. To put it crassly, the "commodity" that is *paraklēsis* belongs to

God, but those who have received it may help pass it on. Moreover, as Paul makes clear, those who have experienced the comfort of God are equipped to comfort those in *any* affliction. Such people offer the comfort of God, poured out into their own life, which the God of all consolation will use to minister to another effectively.

Next, Paul turns his attention to the source of affliction, indicating that the comfort we receive flows to us because we experience the suffering of Christ. "For just as the sufferings of Christ are abundant for us, so also our consolation is abundant through Christ" (2 Cor 1:5). To follow Christ is to participate in his suffering. The 1984 NIV translates "is abundant" (*perisseuō*) as "overflowing," which nicely captures the sense of the verse. "For just as the sufferings of Christ flow over into our lives, so also through Christ our comfort overflows." Those united with Christ cannot avoid the burden of his sufferings, yet they receive the great privilege of his consolation. Both flow naturally from identification with Jesus. But there is a difference. Like a great stream that issues from the very throne of God, the consolation of God flows *through* Jesus to the children of God. It then *overflows* from them into others, pouring forth with life-giving power. Apparently, there is no stopping the flow of God's consolation. This was the good news of 2 Corinthians 1:4.

Paul then moves from an exposition of general principles to speak directly about his own suffering and consolation as well as that of the Corinthian church. He applies what he has just spelled out to their circumstances so the Corinthians might see the benefit that God has produced on their behalf through Paul. "If we are being afflicted, it is for your consolation and salvation; if we are being consoled, it is for your consolation, which you experience when you patiently endure the same sufferings that we are also suffering" (2 Cor 1:6). Here the first-person plural probably refers either to Paul himself (an epistolary plural) or to a small group of companions. Either way, others' experiences of suffering and comfort have direct ramifications for the Corinthians.

No matter whether Paul is experiencing affliction or consolation, the Corinthians benefit. If Paul is experiencing affliction, it guarantees an outpouring of God's consolation, which is meant to be passed on to others. The effects of this consolation are intensified with Paul's inclusion of "salvation." When Paul participates in the suffering of Christ, God's power is unleashed—the power to comfort, console and encourage—and the power to *save*. Here we see the full scope of God's consolation, including God's action to restore and deliver those in need. The consolation and salvation of the Corinthians flow from Paul's own suffering. This mystery will be more fully explored in the final chapter on vicarious suffering. Here it is enough to say that through his affliction Paul is confident of winning lasting change for the Corinthians.

On the other hand, if Paul is experiencing the consolation of God, then the Corinthians too will experience the consolation of God, for Paul knows that he may pass on the consolation he has received in order to edify any who suffer. The NIV's translation of a difficult Greek sequence at the end of the verse is to be preferred to the NRSV: "it is for your comfort, which produces in you patient endurance of the same sufferings we suffer." Here we encounter a further dimension of God's consolation. Because of Paul's affliction and consolation working on behalf of the Corinthians, they will be spiritually equipped to withstand suffering themselves.

It is worth noting that the Corinthians have a history of being reluctant to embrace the necessity of suffering as disciples of Jesus. In fact, they have a history of doubting Paul's authority as an apostle precisely on these grounds. Paul spends much of the first four chapters of 1 Corinthians urging them to recognize that the wisdom of God is revealed in Christ *crucified*. He exhorts the Corinthians to cast aside the world's wisdom and embrace the cruciform life as their own, denying themselves and participating in the way of Jesus. In a scathing indictment of their worldly perspective, Paul speaks with thick sarcasm about their evaluation of his ministry.

> Already you have all you want! Already you have become rich! Quite apart from us you have become kings! Indeed, I wish that you had become kings, so that we might be kings with you! For I think that God has exhibited us apostles as last of all, as though sentenced to death, because we have become a spectacle to the world, to angels and to mortals. We are fools for the sake of Christ, but you are wise in Christ. We are weak, but you are strong. You are held in honor, but we in disrepute. To the present hour we are hungry and thirsty, we are poorly clothed and beaten and homeless, and we grow weary from the work of our own hands. When reviled, we bless; when persecuted, we endure; when slandered, we speak kindly. We have become like the rubbish of the world, the dregs of all things, to this very day. (1 Cor 4:8-13)

The final line in our passage is Paul's expression of his firm hope that the Corinthians will embrace the life of suffering and consolation, with the implication that they too might be ambassadors of consolation to others. "Our hope for you is unshaken; for we know that as you share in our sufferings, so also you share in our consolation" (2 Cor 1:7). The suffering and consolation of life with Christ are not for Paul alone. They are for every disciple of Christ.

To the Corinthians' credit, a passage in 2 Corinthians 7 demonstrates that Paul knew what it meant to receive the consolation of God from them.

> For even when we came into Macedonia, our bodies had no rest, but we were afflicted in every way—disputes without and fears within. But God, who consoles the downcast, consoled

us by the arrival of Titus, and not only by his coming, but also
by the consolation with which he was consoled about you, as
he told us of your longing, your mourning, your zeal for me,
so that I rejoiced still more. (2 Cor 7:5-7)

The consolation of God flows on through all those who experience
suffering (in this case, godly grief and repentance). The Corinthians,
like Paul, could be agents of this comfort. They need only embrace
suffering, receive the promised consolation—and pass it on.

REFLECTIONS

Midway through my first year of seminary I sank into a deep and
dark depression. There seemed to be no escaping the gloom. My
life felt like a prison, my mind a cancer, my soul an open grave. I
longed for death. What was most disconcerting was my own powerlessness. My depression had a life of its own, out of all proportion
with the circumstances of my life. As the months slipped past, I
found myself unable even to assess my depression, let alone respond to it. I was a captive with no hope of rescue. But rescue came.
God delivered me from the darkness through medication, counsel
and the persistent love of those around me, those who hoped for
me when I could no longer hope for myself. God's *paraklēsis* was at
work, comforting and delivering in my hour of need.

It took me three or four years before I could emotionally revisit
those eight months. Now they seem safely a part of my past. The
fear is gone, and the depression itself feels like little more than a
nightmare from which I have woken up. But the *paraklēsis* of God
remains. The consolation that I received, the rescue I experienced—
these have permanently shaped me. They reside within me, waiting
to be passed on to those in need. Occasionally I will find myself
listening to a student pour out a heart filled with grief and despair,
facing giants that are larger than life. Sometimes the situation seems

impossibly difficult with no solution to be found. In such moments I am tempted to think that there is no hope. But then I recall that God breathed hope into me when I was hopeless. He comforted me and delivered me from a consuming darkness. This same comfort is available to all who seek God. I believe that God's comfort can work miracles in the lives of my students. I believe even if they cannot.

As with so many of the ways the Bible looks at suffering, some words of caution are in order as we seek to apply the *paraklēsis* that Paul describes to our own lives. First, I resist the notion that God chooses to submit us to such experiences so that we might be effective ministry tools. I had a student who was convinced that he was molested as a child *so that* he could comfort and encourage others in their own process of healing from similar abuse. I have no doubt that the comfort God has shown him does in fact work to the advantage of others. Nevertheless, we would not hesitate to call an earthly father who used such logic abusive. I see no reason why we should not hold God, the perfect Father, to a similar standard. The consolation Paul speaks of should be viewed as part of God's redemptive work. He takes what is evil and turns it to our good. He takes even the tragedy that befalls us and finds a way to draw us to him. This is what Paul means when he says, "We know that all things work together for good for those who love God, who are called according to his purpose" (Rom 8:28).

A second word of caution is that the comfort of God that we can extend to others is not limited to "shared experience." Paul's idea is not that we must suffer the exact same thing as another person in order to minister to them the hope and comfort of God. What is needed is an experience of deliverance from affliction, comfort in grief, restoration in brokenness. Such experiences remind us of who God is and what he can do. They are a silent testimony of healing and wholeness that enable one to invite God to be present in the pain of another.

The Cruciform Path to Glory

Following God into Suffering

When God gets ahold of our lives, we begin to dream his dreams. My roommate and best friend through college, Matt, was an architecture major. To call UC Berkeley's architecture program rigorous would be an understatement. I watched Matt spend countless hours in the studio working on projects. When deadlines approached, there were nights when I would go to bed before he returned home and wake up to find that he had already left. Sometimes he worked through the night, relying on quick runs to the local coffee shop to keep himself going. He was committed to excellence, and his work showed it. A promising future as an architect seemed to be opening up.

As the years passed and Matt continued to grow into a talented architect, he also continued to grow as a follower of Jesus. Slowly, Jesus was drawing him into partnership with himself, giving him divine perspective on life in the kingdom of God. Over time I saw Matt's dreams change. When we graduated, Matt took a job building affordable community housing in inner-city Oakland with a mission-minded Christian business. In order to have a greater impact on the community they were investing in, the members of the business chose to live in the heart of the city. They understood that reviving a downtrodden community required a commitment of their whole lives. Matt and his wife, Negar, were married in Oakland. They had their children in Oakland. Negar taught in the local elementary school.

Matt and Negar's imagination had been captured by a different vision from the American dream of ease, abundance and prosperity. Instead, their partnership with Jesus led them down the socioeconomic ladder to live and work with the "least of these." It would be foolish to think that Matt and Negar's lives were as easy as they might have been had they made other, "safer" choices, but they would tell you that life in Oakland was filled with God's presence and purpose as they partnered with the King.

PHILIPPIANS 2:5-11

⁵ Let the same mind be in you that was in Christ Jesus,

   ⁶ who, though he was in the form of God,
      did not regard equality with God
      as something to be exploited,
  ⁷ but emptied himself,
      taking the form of a slave,
      being born in human likeness.
And being found in human form,
    ⁸ he humbled himself
      and became obedient to the point of death—
      even death on a cross.

  ⁹ Therefore God also highly exalted him
      and gave him the name
      that is above every name,
  ¹⁰ so that at the name of Jesus
      every knee should bend,
      in heaven and on earth and under the earth,
  ¹¹ and every tongue should confess
      that Jesus Christ is Lord,
      to the glory of God the Father.

This passage provides us with a portrait of the God who suffers, enabling us to see clearly the self-giving love of the Father expressed through his Son. Explicit in this description is the summons to choose this same path of suffering so that we might share the Son's glorious destiny.

The second chapter of Philippians begins with an exhortation for the community to be united, having the "same mind" and the "same love" (Phil 2:2). Paul fleshes this out in the following terms: "Do nothing from selfish ambition or conceit, but in humility regard others as better than yourselves. Let each of you look not [only] to your own interests, but to the interests of others" (Phil 2:3-4). In adopting this attitude, the Philippians are doing nothing less than following the example of Christ their savior. Paul then proceeds to explain the mind and love of Christ, which set the standard for the lives of the Philippians. He does this with the words of an early Christian hymn that may well have been familiar to his audience. This hymn is packed with theology, including an important meditation on God's response to suffering.

Paul introduces the hymn by saying, "Your attitude should be the same as that of Christ Jesus" (Phil 2:6). Structurally, the hymn is connected to this introductory line, making it clear that the hymn is to be seen as paradigmatic for the Philippians. Jesus is their model in all things. The Greek also points backward and evokes the exhortation of Philippians 2:3-4, which the hymn clearly reinforces.

Paul continues: "Who, though he was in the form of God, did not regard equality with God as something to be exploited" (Phil 2:6). Twice this opening line asserts the basic equality of Jesus the Son and God the Father. In fact, the narrative movement of the entire hymn hangs on this assertion. The hymn tells us that Jesus was in the form (*morphē*) of God. We should not read too much into the specific choice of word to describe this oneness. This hymn was composed far in advance of the controversies that raged later in church history over the best way to talk about the unity of Father and Son. In context, it is apparent that the hymn uses the word "form" because it can be used for both sides of a *specific* contrast ("form of God" as opposed to "form of a slave").

Lest we miss the meaning of this first assertion, the hymn tells us that Jesus, who *was* equal with God (*einai isa theō*), did not consider this equality as something to be exploited. To use his position of equality with God to his advantage would have been well within his rights. To garner all of the benefits and glory befitting his status was within his power, but instead Jesus chose a different way. Not exploiting (*harpagmon*) his equality with God means that he did not seek his own gain, his own status, his own privilege, his own glory. To adapt the words of Paul's earlier exhortation to the Philippians, Jesus did nothing from selfish ambition or conceit, but in humility he regarded others as better than himself. He looked not to his own interests but to the interests of others.

The ultimate embodiment of this prioritization of others is the incarnation of Jesus Christ, the great story at the heart of the gospel message. Jesus became flesh and dwelt among us. He "emptied himself, taking the form of a slave, being born in human likeness. And being found in human form [appearance], he humbled himself and became obedient to the point of death—even death on a cross" (2:7-8). Twice the hymn emphasizes the new state that Jesus enters into, reinforcing his true humanity. He is "born in human likeness" and is "found in human appearance." Both convey the remarkable change that Jesus submitted to. This act of "self-emptying" (*auton ekenōsen*) reveals the very heart of God. He who has everything gives everything away on behalf of another. This is the lavish love of God, expressed timelessly in the incarnation.

As a human, Jesus takes the form of a slave. The Creator and Sustainer of all things taking on the form of humanity is already an act of submitting to bondage, but both the life and teaching of Jesus make it clear that there is more at stake here. Jesus did not sweep onto the world stage with power and might at his disposal. His incarnation did not come with fanfare, the blast of trumpets and a victorious military campaign. He was no Alexander the Great; he wasn't even a Herod. He did not descend from the sky; he was born in a manger. He did not grow up teaching and serving in the great temple of his heavenly Father; he wandered the dusty roads of Galilee, a carpenter's son. He emptied himself of *all* status and power and authority. He who was great became lowly.

Once his ministry began, Jesus taught the way of service and self-sacrifice. He taught others the necessity of emptying themselves, of denying themselves, of picking up their crosses and dying for the sake of something greater. He proclaimed that "the Son of Man came not to be served but to serve, and to give his life a ransom for many" (Mk 10:45). "Whoever wishes to become great among you must be your servant, and whoever wishes to be first among you must be slave of all" (Mk 10:43-44). Taking the role of a servant, Jesus washed the disciples' feet, announcing to them, "For I have set you an example, that you also should do as I have done to you" (Jn 13:15). In Jesus, God did not only take the form of humanity. He took the form of a servant, revealing the heart of God for his people in the process.

But Jesus' downward spiral was far from done. The deathless one, God immortal, submitted to death. Such was the emptying of Jesus. Paul makes it clear that such submission was an act of the greatest humility, the same humility that marked every selfless decision made by God on our behalf. This humility once again evokes Paul's initial exhortation to the Philippians. "In humility regard others as better than yourselves" (Phil 2:3). In humility, Jesus placed greater value on our lives than his own. In doing so he was obedient to the will of the Father, who chose to give his Son on our behalf. Thus did Jesus submit to death.

Even this does not mark the nadir of Christ's remarkable self-emptying, for the death he dies is upon a cross. Rejected and scorned by the religious leaders of his own people, abandoned by his closest confidants, mocked by Roman and Jew alike, Jesus, God made man, is put on a cross like a common criminal. He hangs there with a tattered and broken body, having cried out in anguish to a hidden Father, "My God, my God, why have you forsaken me?" (Mk 15:34). He hangs as the ultimate contradiction—the crucified God, the one who gave the law under the curse of the law because he hangs upon a tree, the source of life silenced by death, the one worthy of all honor, glory and praise emptied out to nothing. Nothing.

Already this account has made one thing clear about God. When God looks at suffering, he does not cringe and hide. He does not wave a magic wand and make it go away. Nor is he shamed by the scandal of affliction that takes place under his watch. Rather, the will of God seems to go right *through* suffering. He *chooses* for it. But why? That is what the rest of the hymn makes clear.

The next verse marks the great turning point in the hymn. "Therefore God also highly exalted him and gave him the name that is above every name" (Phil 2:9). Precisely *because* Jesus emptied himself in this fashion, God acts on his behalf, exalting him to the highest place. God's power raises Jesus from the dead, establishing him as the firstfruits of the resurrection. He ascends into heaven and takes his place at the right hand of the Father, the "highest place." His sacrifice and suffering on our behalf establish him as the mediator of salvation. As such, he has the name above every name, Lord Jesus, the only name by which we are saved.

All of this is apparent to the Philippians already. It is the good news that they have believed, and it is why they have given Jesus their allegiance. Yet it is just the beginning of God's vindication of his Son. Jesus' exaltation by God awaits a final movement in which the Philippians will participate: "So that at the name of Jesus every knee should bend, in heaven and on earth and under the earth, and every tongue should confess that Jesus Christ is Lord, to the glory of God the Father" (Phil 2:10-11). Jesus, with all the authority of God himself, will return to establish his dominion over all of creation. The reality of Jesus' exaltation, which is currently embraced by a persecuted few, will be revealed in a manner that compels universal acknowledgment. His authority will know no bounds. Friends and enemies alike will take a knee on that day, acknowledging Jesus' power and authority. Every person and power in heaven, on earth and under the earth will submit to Jesus. His dominion will be complete.

These last phrases purposefully recall an important text from the prophet Isaiah. "Turn to me and be saved, all the ends of the earth! For I am God, and there is no other. By myself I have sworn, from my mouth has gone forth in righteousness a word that shall not return: 'To me every knee shall bow, every tongue shall swear'" (Is 45:22-23). By evoking this text, Paul makes the full extent of Christ's exaltation clear. The one who was equal to God in the beginning is declared "Lord" in the sense that only God is Lord. The glory of God belongs to Jesus. The authority of God belongs to Jesus. The salvation of God comes through Jesus. In the context of Isaiah 45, to confess that every knee will bow and every tongue will confess the authority of Jesus is to confess that Jesus and the Father are one. The hymn has come full circle. The one who emptied himself has been filled with the full measure of God. In the process, he has made possible a new hope for all those who would follow him. But there is more: Jesus is also changed. In his resurrected body, he will continue his identification with us for the rest of eternity. He has become our high priest, the great reconciler whose faithfulness to the Father paves the way for the renewal of all things.

Do not miss the political and religious overtones of the declaration. Just as Isaiah denounced the various idols that Israel called

"Lord," asserting that they were nothing more than blocks of wood (Is 45:20), so also Paul addresses all those who would usurp the title that belongs to God alone. Chief among the culprits was the Roman Caesar, who claimed the title "Lord" for himself.

This hymn summarizes the principal movements of the gospel narrative: preexistence, incarnation, ministry, death, resurrection, ascension and parousia. All of this magnifies the glory of God the Father. God's glory has been enhanced by the emptying of his Son. The demonstration of Jesus' selfless love has revealed him to be worthy of worship. Just as Jesus taught, he who became least is indeed made first. He who made himself the slave of all is called Lord by all. Likewise, the exaltation of his Son brings glory to the Father, who is able to restore Jesus to his rightful place of honor and authority, revealing him to be Lord over all and one with the Father.

The spectacle of Christ's dramatic descent and ascent should not distract us from Paul's reason for evoking the example of Jesus. The hymn tells the story of Jesus so that the Philippians might have the same mind as Jesus. The life of Jesus is paradigmatic for the life of believers everywhere. If Jesus emptied himself, the Philippians are to empty themselves. If Jesus chose the path of suffering and self-denial, the Philippians are to choose the path of suffering and self-denial. If Jesus did nothing from selfish ambition or conceit, but in humility regarded others as better than himself, the Philippians should do likewise. If Jesus looked not to his own interests but to the interests of others, the Philippians should follow his lead.

The promise is that if they do, they too will be exalted by God. They will partake in the glory of the resurrected Christ. "He will transform the body of our humiliation that it may be conformed to the body of his glory" (Phil 3:21). The path to glory has been marked out for us by God. What is revealed in Jesus is that the path to glory is a cruciform path, defined by suffering and self-denial, service and sacrifice, humility and love of others. As Paul says later, "I want to know Christ and the power of his resurrection and the sharing of his sufferings by becoming like him in his death, if somehow I may attain the resurrection from the dead" (Phil 3:10-11).

What, then, have we learned about suffering? Philippians 2:5-11 offers us three critical insights that expand our theological horizons. First, we see that God is a suffering God. However great the mystery of suffering may remain, it is clear that God himself chose to experience all of the afflictions common to humans— and so much more! We should take comfort knowing that the God whom we call upon in times of need has been in the dark valley as well. He has known pain, shame and rejection. He has experienced loss in ways that we cannot imagine. In our suffering he is never far off. He is the one who truly draws near. Our inclination is to assume God's absence in the midst of suffering, but Jesus shows us that nothing could be further from the truth. He has shown himself to be Immanuel, God with us, in sorrow and joy, suffering and glory.

Second, God has revealed in his Son the only way to share in his glory. Just as Jesus submitted to suffering in order to realize our salvation and receive his own glorious inheritance, so too we must be willing to tread the hard path of suffering, walking in our Savior's steps. As Jesus reminded his followers, "A disciple is not above the teacher, nor a slave above the master; it is enough for the disciple to be like the teacher, and the slave like the master" (Mt 10:24-25).

Third, we learn that the reward is indeed great. If Jesus' suffering and exaltation are paradigmatic for the believer, the good news is that God will reward the sacrifices of the disciple. The one who joins with Jesus in self-emptying will be joined with Jesus in his glory. Suffering ultimately has a destination other than loss; the more one loses, the more one will gain from God. Humility results in exaltation. Suffering results in vindication. Self-sacrifice results in glory. Such glory is impossible to measure. "For this slight momentary affliction is preparing us for an eternal weight of glory beyond all measure" (2 Cor 4:17).

REFLECTIONS

Churches are often reticent to talk about the cruciform path to glory. Blessing, prosperity and joy—these are the things our teachers and leaders promise us. Perhaps it is because these are the promises that fill the pews and the offering plate. Rarely are we called to count the cost of discipleship, to take a good long look at the life of Jesus. What we find there makes us uncomfortable. He tells us that he must lose his life and that we must lose ours as well. He tells us that he must take up his cross and that we must take up ours as well. Our path is joined to his. We are destined to walk as he walked, sharing in his trials and tribulations as well as his victory.

Ironically, lack of ambition is one of the impediments to embracing Jesus' cruciform path to glory. We tend to think of ambition as a less-than-worthy attribute for a disciple, yet Jesus often speaks of reward. For example, he tells the young man who idolizes his wealth to abandon it so that he might have "treasure in heaven" (Mk 10:21). In the Sermon on the Mount he exhorts his hearers to practice prayer, almsgiving and fasting for God alone so that they may be "rewarded" by God (Mt 6:4, 6, 18). He consistently speaks of those who will be first and last in the estimation of the kingdom of God (three times in Mark alone! Mk 9:35; 10:31; 10:44). James and John do not yet understand the path of Jesus when they approach him and ask to sit at his right and left in his glory, but Jesus does not rebuke them for their desire to be great. He does not tell them that ambition is a trait unworthy of the kingdom. Rather, he seeks to redirect their ambition. True greatness, esteem in the kingdom of God, is achieved through service. "Whoever wishes to become great among you must be your servant, and whoever wishes to be first among you must be slave of all" (Mk 10:43-44). The logic of the Philippian hymn only works if believers cultivate the desire to be great—not great in the ways of the world (fame, fortune, power, success and beauty), but great in the kingdom of God, sharing in the suffering of Jesus so that we might participate in his glory. As Hebrews says, we should look to Jesus, "who for the sake of the joy that was set before him endured the cross, disregarding its shame, and has taken his seat at the right hand of the throne of God" (Heb 12:2).

One of my favorite examples of conforming to the self-emptying nature of Jesus is St. Francis of Assisi. Francis was born into a wealthy family in medieval Italy. As a young man he earned quite a reputation for prodigality and mischief, but he also had a tender heart. When God captured that tender heart, Francis surrendered himself to his heavenly Father with remarkable faith. Francis was particularly drawn to care for the marginalized, giving lavishly to the poor and ministering to lepers. One turning point in Francis' life came when his father, the wealthy silk merchant Pietro Bernadone, dragged his son before the local bishop, determined to put an end to his outrageous acts of generosity and recover something of the funds Francis had squandered on the poor. Francis courageously stood before the bishop and formally renounced any claim to his father's estate. He then shocked the whole assembly by stripping off his clothes and handing them to his father. Standing naked before him, Francis professed, "Until now I called you my father, but from now on I can say without reserve, 'Our Father who art in heaven.' He is all my wealth and I place all my confidence in him." With this act, Francis unequivocally declared his commitment to a life of poverty, having cast aside the final safety net. He chose solidarity with the poor and unwavering reliance on God, and great was his reward. A deep communion with God defined Francis's life. The stories of his later life and ministry are inspiring. God used him powerfully as a reformer, miracle worker, evangelist, diplomat, missionary, teacher and theologian. Years after his death, Francis's life remains a poignant reminder that God glorifies those who embrace the cruciform path.

To Suffer for Another

*Participation in the
Suffering of God*

Between 1940 and 1944, the small Protestant French village of Le
Chambon-sur-Lignon sheltered an estimated 5,000 people (mostly
Jews) who were being rounded up for extermination by the Nazis
and the French puppet government in Vichy. The village of 5,000
embraced danger and hardship in order to care for these strangers.
They made false documents for their guests and integrated them
into village life in order to project an image of normalcy. Led by
their pastors and emboldened by their faith, the community stood
together in their resolve to help as many people as they could. This
solidarity proved instrumental in keeping the authorities at bay, but
discovery and retaliation were ever-present possibilities. The inhabitants of Le Chambon took these risks because they were committed to Jesus, who called them to love their neighbor as themselves. In 1943, the two most influential pastors and the headmaster
of the local primary school were sent to a work camp for 28 days.
They were fortunate to leave the camp alive. Others paid a greater
price, including a teacher and the village physician, both of whom
were executed by the SS for sheltering Jews.

COLOSSIANS 1:24

> [24] I am now rejoicing in my sufferings for your sake, and in my flesh I am completing what is lacking in Christ's afflictions for the sake of his body, that is, the church.

In the last chapter we saw that Christ has shown the path to glory lies through suffering. He walked that path himself and calls each of us to follow in his footsteps. Colossians 1:24 takes this idea a step further. The key to understanding this text is to grasp the degree of Paul's identification with Christ. The mystery of union with God accomplished through Christ lies at the very heart of his theology. He consistently describes his life, ministry, calling and of course suffering in terms of participation in the life of Christ. As he says in Galatians, "I have been crucified with Christ; and it is no longer I who live, but it is Christ who lives in me. And the life I now live in the flesh I live by faith in the Son of God, who loved me and gave himself for me" (Gal 2:19-20). This is more than mere allegiance. Paul is convinced that he shares in the life of Christ and that Christ lives through him. This union extends to the whole church. Paul thinks of the church as the very body of Christ, God's own hands and feet in the world. The community of faith is also the new temple of God, with the Holy Spirit taking up residence inside its members. Both of these images are Paul's attempts to make intelligible the mysterious union between the church and Christ that now defines God's people.

With this in mind, let us turn to our passage. As always, the context is significant. In Colossians 1:15-19, Paul proclaims the absolute supremacy of Christ. He is the source of all creation, and it finds its purpose in him. Paul then singles out the church, which shares an even more intimate bond with Christ: "He is the head of the body, the church; he is the beginning, the firstborn from the dead" (Col 1:18). Next Paul talks about the reconciling work accomplished by God in Christ. He begins with the reconciliation of creation: "God was pleased to reconcile to himself all things, whether on earth or in heaven, by making peace through the blood of his cross" (Col 1:20). He then singles out the church again, reminding the Colossian Christians of their new identity in Christ. "And you who were once estranged and hostile in mind, doing evil deeds, he has now reconciled in his fleshly body through death, so as to present you holy and blameless and irreproachable before him" (Col 1:21-22). As a "servant of this gospel," Paul himself has become part of this reconciling work (Col 1:23).

The first phrase in our key text, Colossians 1:24, begins with the word *nun* ("now"). This is almost certainly a nod to the great truths Paul has just proclaimed. In short, Paul is telling his audience that he rejoices in his sufferings for their sake because of the greatness of God's redemptive work and Paul's absolute commitment to it as a servant.

It is not unheard of for Paul to rejoice in his sufferings. We have already seen that Paul has a much deeper sense of what suffering can accomplish than most of us. Nevertheless, as verse 24 unfolds it becomes clear that there is a different nuance present here. To begin with, Paul claims that he rejoices in suffering that he undertakes "for your sake" or "on your behalf" (*hyper hymōn*). There is a vicarious dimension to Paul's suffering; his suffering accomplishes something positive for the Colossian Christians. Christ is, of course, the ultimate example of vicarious suffering. He bore the punishment for our sins to pave the way for our reconciliation. He became the Suffering Servant described in Isaiah:

> Surely he has borne our infirmities
>   and carried our diseases;
> yet we accounted him stricken,
>   struck down by God, and afflicted.

But he was wounded for our transgressions,
>   crushed for out iniquities;
upon him was the punishment that made us whole,
>   and by his bruises we are healed.
All we like sheep have gone astray;
>   we have all turned to our own way,
and the LORD has laid on him
>   the iniquity of us all. (Is 53:4-6)

What is Paul's suffering accomplishing for the Colossian Christians? While preaching the gospel, Paul was imprisoned, flogged, shipwrecked, stoned, hungry and naked (2 Cor 11:23-27). But his gospel proclamation also brought the reconciliation of God to those in desperate need, including the Colossian Christians. Paul knows through experience that you cannot have one without the other. "For we are the aroma of Christ to God among those who are being saved and among those who are perishing; to the one a fragrance from death to death, to the other a fragrance from life to life" (2 Cor 2:15-16). As a servant of the gospel, Paul has experienced both of these responses firsthand. He knows full well that contempt, disdain, anger and violence will follow close behind his kingdom proclamation, but he embraces them all for the sake of those who will be reconciled to God.

The second half of Colossians 1:24 carries the vicarious dimension of Paul's suffering even further: "And in my flesh I am completing what is lacking in Christ's afflictions for the sake of his body, that is, the church." The chief puzzle in this verse involves Paul's assertion that something is "lacking in Christ's afflictions" that needs completing. Before trying to unpack Paul's meaning in this verse, it is important to clarify what Paul *doesn't* mean. This is not a statement about the inadequacy of Jesus' atoning sacrifice. Paul's entire theology of salvation is predicated on the sufficiency of Christ's sacrifice. In fact, we have just heard him speak of the universal scope of reconciliation accomplished by Christ in Colossians 1:20-22. In short, Jesus has paid the penalty for sin once and for all on the cross. What, then, is lacking that Paul's own suffering completes?

Paul's eschatology is front and center here, and particularly his grasp of the "already and not yet" of the kingdom. As we saw in chapter 7, the ministry, death and resurrection of Jesus inaugurated the kingdom of God. The redemption of humanity and creation has begun in earnest. This reconciling work is made possible by Jesus' death on the cross and validated by his subsequent resurrection by the Father. However, we currently live between the ages, *already* experiencing the fruit of the age to come while *not yet* experiencing its fullness. Paul's assertion that he fills up what is lacking in Christ's afflictions takes this reality seriously. Paul and others like him have entered into renewed relationship with God through Christ, but the tyranny of suffering, sin and death remain very real. Suffering coexists with salvation as we wait for the final redemption of all things.

Though the penalty for sin was paid on the cross, Christ continues to suffer for his people, the church. He walks with them in persecution and hardship, bearing their burdens. He suffers when Alice doesn't have enough to eat. He suffers when Tom's body is ravaged by cancer. He suffers when Cameron's wife leaves him for another man. He suffers when Lacy loses her friends because she became a Christian. As long as the world remains broken, Jesus will suffer on behalf of his church. But Jesus also suffers for those who are not yet part of his church. He patiently suffers with the sorrows of the world because he longs for more people to be saved. He takes up the world's pain and grief and despair and exchanges it for hope. This is the tension of the already and not yet. The whole of creation groans for Jesus to return and set all things right, but God longs for as many as possible to find their way to the church before that day comes.

In short, what is lacking in Christ's afflictions are the unfolding sufferings of this present age. As long as suffering, sin and death persist, the Suffering Servant will continue to bear their weight. The church was ransomed from the power of darkness on the cross, God's promise of forgiveness secured for all generations, but the Suffering Servant continues to bear a burden.

Paul recognizes that he has a pivotal role to play in these sufferings. If his life has been joined to Christ's and the life he lives is lived through Christ, then he takes part in the vicarious suffering of his Savior. In fact, he is in an ideal position to experience this suffering since he can bear it in the flesh in a way that the risen Jesus himself no longer can. Just as he has the privilege of announcing the kingdom as Jesus' mouthpiece and ministering as Jesus' hands and feet, Paul also recognizes that he will suffer with God on behalf of his people. Paul rejoices that he can share in this with Jesus. It is part of his participation in the life of Christ, his complete identification with the Suffering Servant whose gospel he proclaims.

REFLECTIONS

Christians unite themselves with Jesus and consequently share in the life of God. This mysterious union means that Jesus is more than just our example. He lives in us and we live through him. This means that we are reminded once again that God suffers. He suffers on behalf of others. He suffered for us when he took on flesh and made himself susceptible to frailty and sorrow and death. He suffered for us when he paid the penalty of sin on the cross. Every day that the return of Christ is put off involves suffering for God. Instead of putting a final end to sin and suffering and death, he waits patiently for the fullness of the church to be gathered to himself. In the meantime, he continues to intercede for his people, walking with them in the midst of pain, loss, guilt and death. In fact, our union with him enables him to bear the burdens of the church. In our moment of despair, we ought to heed the words of the psalmist: "Cast your burden on the LORD, and he will sustain you; he will never permit the righteous to be moved" (Ps 55:22). Thank God we never suffer alone.

This mystery deepens with the understanding that those who belong to God actually share in God's vicarious suffering. Though we obviously do not pay the debt of sin, we do suffer on behalf of others. Let me highlight three ways this happens.

First, members of Christ's body are called to identify with each other in all things. Paul tells the Roman church to "rejoice with those who rejoice, weep with those who weep" (Rom 12:15). If one member is suffering, the whole community suffers. This solidarity is born out of our union in Christ. Similarly, Paul instructs the Galatians to "bear one another's burdens, and in this way you will fulfill the law of Christ" (Gal 6:2). My wife served as a hospital chaplain for a number of years. Through her stories I became profoundly aware of our basic human need to have others bear our burdens. Her great privilege was to represent Christ to those in turmoil. She bore witness to their pain. She gave voice to their prayers. She shared in the tears and the groans and the questions. She would come home exhausted and spent—and yet full of life.

Second, we suffer on behalf of another when we engage in any form of incarnational ministry. To meet others where they are means laying down our own familiarity, comfort, rights and freedoms. Missionaries who go overseas suffer the death of one life in order to embrace another. They open themselves to a new community, a new language and a new culture. Much like Jesus, who chose to become one of us, these missionaries give up what they know and cherish for the sake of another. My church supports a number of overseas missionaries, including a family that has spent most of the last two decades in Japan. Japan is a difficult mission field, requiring an investment in relationship that may span years before there is enough trust to have fruitful conversations about Jesus. This family's entire reality has been shaped by the choice to leave what was familiar and follow God's call to Japan.

Finally, the very fact that we wait for the consummation of all things entails its own kind of suffering. Those who share in the life of God have already tasted the goodness of the coming kingdom. Consequently, they groan for the glorious future that will arrive with Jesus' return. Waiting on this future, especially when the present age remains filled with pain and sorrow, entails its own kind of suffering, a necessary patience in the face of deep longing. We are able to bear with the frustration and futility of this present age because we know that it benefits others, particularly those outside the church. Jesus has not yet returned because he wants to draw more people to himself. We have our own role to play in this mission. So we must make the most of the time allotted to us in the "already and not yet," patiently waiting to be called home, first to Christ in the heavens and ultimately to a renewed earth and a resurrected body. As Paul says, "For to me, living is Christ and dying is gain. If I am to live in the flesh, that means fruitful labor for me; and I do not know which I prefer. I am hard pressed between the two: my desire is to depart and be with Christ, for that is far better; but to remain in the flesh is more necessary for you" (Phil 1:21-24). The fact is that, if we are participating in Christ's life, we will be faced with a thousand opportunities to suffer and sacrifice for the sake of another.

- 14 -

Conclusion

✝

Like a banquet spread before us, these twelve passages reveal a variety of meaningful ways to engage the problem of suffering. We have seen that each of these responses offers us something unique that needs to be taken seriously as we wrestle with suffering. I would like to close by making five observations that emerge from our study.

Taking the Options Seriously

First, if we are to follow the Bible's lead as we struggle with suffering, we must cultivate an awareness and openness to the breadth of responses we see within it. I began this exploration of the Bible's response to suffering by insisting that a one-size-fits-all approach did not do justice to what we find in the Bible. Rather than trumpeting a single "correct" way to approach suffering, the Bible presents us with a complex web of possibilities. Some of these approaches are mutually exclusive, but many are capable of being woven together, increasing the complexity of the harmony that is the Bible's response to suffering.

1. Deuteronomy 30:15-20 opened up the possibility that suffering may be punishment from God. With an emphasis on

God's justice, the "two ways" encountered in this passage highlights God's commitment to bless the righteous and condemn the wicked.

2. In Genesis 4:1-8, the story of Cain and Abel reminded us that much suffering results from the sinful choices of others. Evidence of humanity's rebellion against God is on display in every generation, and many innocents pay the price.

3. In Genesis 45:4-8, Joseph's many misfortunes revealed that God's redemptive power is stronger than the suffering that afflicts us. He can take even the most evil acts and use them to further his own purposes for good.

4. Luke 22:31-34 gave us insight into the work of Satan, who used suffering and fear to cause Peter to fall away from Jesus. We are called to resist the enemy, confident that God is greater than our adversary. As he did with Peter, we must remember that he has the power to rescue us even when we fall.

5. In Job 40:8-14, God spoke to Job out of the whirlwind, reminding him of his great power and wisdom. Faced with the terrible otherness of God, Job surrendered to God and accepted the mystery of suffering. He was able to do so because God did not remain distant, but made himself known.

6. Romans 8:18-25 set our present suffering within the context of God's redemptive purposes. We are invited to take part in God's great story, partnering with him here and now to advance the kingdom in joyful anticipation of his return, when we will rejoice with all of creation as we are set free from suffering and decay.

7. In Hebrews 12:1-13 we saw that suffering, though never welcome, can play an important role in our spiritual growth and development, shaping us in Christlikeness through training.

Ultimately, suffering is not only loss. It also contains the seeds of opportunity. Suffering is sometimes like the lodgepole pine, whose pinecones open up and release their seeds in the extreme temperatures of a forest fire. Mysteriously, there is new life to be found in some suffering.

8. Exodus 17:1-7 showed us that God can use suffering to test our faith as he did with the wilderness generation. Such testing reveals the quality of our faith. Moreover, the tests also provide an opportunity for God to act on our behalf, growing our faith even as it is tested.

9. In 2 Corinthians 4:7-12, Paul turned the tables on our perception of weakness and frailty. God's power and grace are more evident when he works through these clay jars. Even more remarkably, the power of God's new life is made known through us as we embrace suffering in solidarity with Christ in his death.

10. In 2 Corinthians 1:3-7, we were reminded that God is our comforter in the midst of suffering. This comfort not only ministers to us in sorrow and pain, it also becomes available to others through us.

11. The great hymn to Christ in Philippians 2:5-11 taught us to model our lives after the life of Jesus, whose suffering, service and sacrifice for our sake was rewarded with glory and honor by God. We are invited to join him in emptying ourselves for the sake of others so that we might also share in his glory.

12. Finally, Colossians 1:24 urged us to participate in God's own suffering as it unfolds in the already and not yet. The people of God—all those who unite themselves with him and participate in the advancement of his kingdom—will suffer the wounds of a world waiting for new creation.

THE NECESSITY OF DISCERNMENT

This leads to a second observation. Since we are confronted by twelve distinct biblical approaches to suffering, how are we to discern which of the twelve applies in any particular instance of suffering? It would be wonderful if this discernment process were simple and straightforward. Our temptation is to match up the biblical responses with particular life scenarios, creating a mammoth spreadsheet that covers every eventuality and provides a divinely sanctioned answer: Cancer equals testing. Depression equals training. Murder equals free will. Such an approach is doomed to failure because it tries to flatten out the variables of God, self and circumstances.

The drive for this kind of clarity and certainty is like the Pharisees' approach to the Old Testament law. In their approach to the Sabbath, for instance, the drive to define what exactly constituted "work" led them to create extensive lists of forbidden and acceptable practices. Their desire to get it "right" ultimately rendered them unable to let God tell them what Sabbath observance should look like. The first rule of discernment is that the insight we seek is found in God. There are no formulas to replace his wisdom.

How, then, are we to go about the process of discernment? The first gift God has given us is Scripture itself. Simply being familiar with the variety of approaches the Bible takes to suffering gives us good categories to work with. We are not left to cast about in the dark, drawing any conclusion we want. God has given us a range of meaningful and appropriate possibilities. Approaches to suffering that stray from these possibilities depart from the path of wisdom. Perhaps most noteworthy, no biblical approaches ever compromise God's goodness or his power.

Alongside Scripture, God has given us community. We were created to live in community with other believers, and God often uses other people to help us come to grips with our pain. When we live life openly and authentically with others, the brothers and sisters with whom we share our lives are in a unique position to help us understand the suffering we experience. In fact, they may be better able to interpret our suffering when our own perspective is clouded by pain and sorrow. They may lead us into repentance, enable us to cast off false guilt, help us to hope for a better future, embody the consolation of God in our moment of grief, or guide us into any one of the other biblical responses to suffering. My wife, Julie, and I were in the early stages of a dating relationship when I began to sink into the deep depression I spoke of in chapter 11. She proved an invaluable companion as I fought my way through the fog of sorrow and pain. Not only did she extend God's grace and compassion to me, she also offered me perspective that was quite simply beyond me, helping me discern truth and falsehood when my world was turned upside down. Of course, for others to play this key role in the discernment process they must be walking with God and listening to him. This brings us to the ultimate source for discerning the appropriate response to suffering: God himself.

God's Spirit lives within every believer. He has drawn near to us and made us his beloved children. He is eager for us to pray to him, lifting up our questions, desires and concerns. But we also need to listen. We need to open our hearts and minds to his wisdom. We need to turn to him when we are coming to grips with the suffering in our lives, trusting that he will make clear to us what we need to know.

One benefit of suffering is that it makes our own lack of control abundantly clear. When we are being crushed in the vise of suffering, we certainly need God to act if we are to find a way out, but our dependence runs even deeper than that. We need God to speak if we are to make any sense of our suffering. We need his Spirit to do what only he can: tell us the source and appropriate response to our suffering. God alone can show us if our suffering is punishment intended to elicit repentance. Only he can make it clear when our suffering is being woven into his divine purposes. God may tell us that, in order to understand our suffering, we need look no further than the sinful choices of humanity and the broken world those choices have produced. When Satan seeks to separate us from our heavenly Father, it is God who encourages us to direct our struggle against our spiritual enemy. When the sorrows of life threaten to consume us, God remains God, a source of life and hope even if we can't understand anything else. God is the one who reminds us that our personal stories and the story of the whole world belong to him, and it is God alone who has the power to bring that story to its promised climax. God must show us when our suffering is training in the life of faith, and God must show us when it is testing intended to reveal the quality of that faith. God makes plain when we are to rejoice in our weaknesses, opening our eyes to see how he will step into the breach. God alone can offer us a comfort that surpasses understanding, and he enables us to share that comfort with others. It is God who shows us when we are to pick up our crosses and deny ourselves, following in the footsteps of our master. He alone has the power to exalt us when we empty ourselves. Lastly, it is God who invites us to share in his own suffering, participating with him in the reconciliation of the world. There is no formula for discernment, but God has promised to lead his children through the valley. He will reveal to us what we need to know. We must take him at his word when he says, "Ask, and it will be given you; search and you will find; knock and the door will be opened for you. For everyone who asks receives, and everyone who searches finds, and for everyone who knocks, the door will be opened" (Mt 7:7-8).

Embracing Mystery

A third observation that arises from contemplating the Bible's twelve approaches to suffering is that these approaches, in spite of the fact that the Bible clearly has a lot to say about suffering, still involve a great degree of mystery. We are in a better place than we would be without these approaches, but none of them affords us absolute clarity. At some point we must come to peace with the things we can know and the things that are simply beyond us. There is always a degree to which suffering will remain a mystery to us. I raise this as an important takeaway because so many of us are frankly dissatisfied with partial understanding. We doubt that truth can be bigger than we are. Mystery seems like a cop-out.

For this reason, the problem of suffering presents us with the greatest challenge of trust. Will we not only seek God for answers, trusting him to reveal what we need to know, but also trust him with the questions that remain? Though God has revealed himself to us, he also remains hidden. In this life, we will never know as God knows. As Paul reminds us, "For now we see in a mirror, dimly, but then we will see face to face. Now I know only in part; then I will know fully, even as I have been fully known" (1 Cor 13:12). For now, we are called to trust in God, particularly with those elements of our suffering that remain shrouded in mystery.

ACCEPTING THE PROCESS

Fourth, as important as these twelve biblical responses to suffering may be, we are not always ready to receive them. Grief, loss and pain can be disorienting and all-consuming. We often need time to come to grips with the suffering that has engulfed us. Most of us know from experience that the best thing we can do for others when they are first plunged into suffering is simply to be present with them and listen to the groaning of their hearts. We need to resist the urge to "solve" their problems or "interpret" their suffering. It is enough to honor their pain.

Over the course of a year, Nicholas Wolterstorff recorded his thoughts and feelings about the loss of his adult son, who died in a tragic climbing accident. These reflections became a wonderful book, *Lament for a Son*. In the first portion of the book, with the grief and pain so close, Wolterstorff is rightly inconsolable. Many of the biblical responses to suffering strike him as hollow and dissatisfying—even the future resurrection of his son, which he continues to affirm. The wisdom offered by those around him ends up sounding trite at best. At worst, it diminishes the reality of his pain and the worth of his son.

Wolterstorff helps us to see that coming to grips with suffering is always a process. As we slowly learn to live with suffering, the time will necessarily come when we will wrestle with God's perspective on our suffering. When we arrive at this point, understanding what the Bible says about suffering and diligently seeking the wisdom of God become invaluable tools as we move forward with him. We see this transition play out in *Lament for a Son*. As the book progresses, Wolterstorff finds meaning in a variety of biblical responses to suffering. For instance he writes, "In the valley of suffering, despair and bitterness are brewed. But there also character is made. The valley of suffering is the vale of soul-making." This is the kind of conclusion that we must grow into. Though the Bible talks in similar terms, the notion that one's spiritual growth can be enhanced by the death of a son sounds callous and cruel, especially when the wound is still fresh. The truth is, of course, more complicated. The connection between suffering and soul-making remains full of mystery. Wolterstorff recognizes this tension. "How do I sustain my 'No' to my son's early death while accepting with gratitude the opportunity offered of becoming what otherwise I could never be? How do I receive my suffering as blessing while repulsing the obscene thought that God jiggled the mountain to make *me* better?"

Wolterstorff's reflection sums up a paradox that runs throughout the Bible's treatment of suffering. On the one hand, our twelve texts never make suffering into something that it is not. Suffering is painful and difficult, even in those instances when it comes from God (as an extension of his justice, as training or a test). On the other hand, our texts reveal to us a God who is greater than our suffering. He is powerful, creative and committed to his creation. He always has the last word. In fact, time and time again God has the amazing capacity to accomplish his purposes through suffering.

If receptivity to many of the Bible's approaches to suffering only emerges with the passing of time, then this creates an additional challenge for those who would give pastoral care. Knowing the variety of biblical responses to suffering is a good starting point, but we would be fools to think that we can simply dispense them like medicine. We must look to God and follow his lead as we discern *which* biblical responses to suffering are appropriate and *when* to raise them with a hurting friend. I would like to emphasize that many of the responses explored in this book may come across as cold and unfeeling when shared with someone still struggling with great loss. They may well seem like attempts to make the pain seem "worthwhile." In pastoral situations, I would urge great patience and restraint. Don't jump to conclusions or offer simplistic answers. Always begin with the ministry of presence and let God take the lead in unpacking deeper truths.

RENEWING HOPE

Finally, each of our twelve biblical responses to suffering reminds us of the importance of hope. Suffering seeks to dominate us. Physically, emotionally, socially and spiritually, suffering screams at us, demanding our complete attention. In large part this is for our own good. Suffering signals us that something is terribly wrong, and it demands that we act in order to address the crisis. Suffering may be painful, but it does orient us to the truth. The problem is that suffering can be so consuming that it crowds out hope, and hope is essential in dealing with our suffering. Hope reminds us that God is at work, that with his help our future holds more than pain, loss and sorrow. Hope opens the door to new possibilities. It enables us to reimagine our past, present and future in light of God, who loves us, seeks our good and remains powerful in the midst of our suffering.

Each of these biblical responses to suffering draws us back to God. Together they encourage us to seek him in the midst of our suffering so that hope may be reborn. This hope holds tight to the convictions that God is bigger than our suffering and he is at work in our lives even as the flames engulf us. He will fight for us, comfort us, refine us, establish us, partner with us and, ultimately, save us.

> "See, the home of God is among mortals.
> He will dwell with them:
> they will be his peoples,
> and God himself will be with them;
> he will wipe every tear from their eyes.
> Death will be no more;
> mourning and crying and pain will be no more,
> for the first things have passed away."

And the one who was seated on the throne said, "See, I am making all things new." (Rev 21:3-5)

Notes

INTRODUCTION

p. 12   *The problem of suffering has haunted me*: Bart Ehrman, *God's Problem: How the Bible Fails to Answer Our Most Important Question—Why We Suffer* (New York: Harper-Collins, 2008), 1.

p. 13   *Not that I am (I think) in much real danger*: C. S. Lewis, *A Grief Observed* (New York: HarperCollins, 1961), 5.

p. 13   *Are you capable of forgiving and loving God*: Harold S. Kushner, *When Bad Things Happen to Good People* (New York: Schocken Books, 1981), 148.

CHAPTER FIVE: THE ACCUSER

p. 67   *There are two equal and opposite errors*: C. S. Lewis, *The Screwtape Letters* (San Francisco: HarperSanFrancisco, 2001), ix.

CHAPTER EIGHT: RUNNING THE RACE

p. 92   *Well, I don't know what will happen now*: For the full text of King's last speech, see *King Institute Encyclopedia*, "I've Been to the Mountaintop," http://kingencyclopedia .stanford.edu/encyclopedia/documentsentry/ive_been _to_the_mountaintop.1.html

p. 102   *He has paid us the intolerable compliment*: C. S. Lewis, *The Problem of Pain* (New York: Macmillan, 1974), 41.

pp. 103-4   *One night toward the end of January*: Martin Luther King Jr., *Stride Toward Freedom: The Montgomery Story* (Boston: Beacon, 2010), 124-25.

p. 105   *It was to me a very grave matter*: J. Hudson Taylor, *Hudson Taylor* (Minneapolis: Bethany House, 1987), 21-22.

Chapter Ten: Jars of Clay

p. 128   *Before my accident, I didn't 'need' Christ*: Joni Eareckson and Joe Musser, *Joni* (Grand Rapids: Zondervan, 1976), 110.

Chapter Twelve: The Cruciform Path to Glory

p. 149   *Until now I called you my father*: Marion H. Habig, ed., *St. Francis of Assisi: Writings and Early Biographies: English Omnibus of the Sources for the Life of St. Francis* (Chicago: Franciscan Herald Press, 1973), 643.

Conclusion

p. 166   *In the valley of suffering, despair and bitterness are brewed*: Nicholas Wolterstorff, *Lament for a Son* (Grand Rapids: Eerdmans, 1987), 97.

p. 166   *How do I sustain my 'No'*: Ibid.

Subject Index

Scripture Index

Finding the Textbook You Need

The IVP Academic Textbook Selector
is an online tool for instantly finding the IVP books
suitable for over 250 courses across 24 disciplines.

www.ivpress.com/academic/